THE HOLY SPIRIT

AN INTRODUCTION

The Holy Spirit

An Introduction

David Petts

Published by Mattersey Hall, Mattersey,
DN10 5HD. England.

ISBN 1 873324 03 0

Printed by: MFP Design & Print,
Unit E3, Longford Trading Estate,
Thomas Street, Stretford,
Manchester. M32 0JT.
Tel: 0161-864 4540
Fax: 0161-866 9866

Publisher's Note

Mattersey Hall is an international, evangelical Bible College with an emphasis that is distinctly charismatic. Students are drawn from a wide variety of nations, denominations, and fellowships. The College is owned by Assemblies of God, one of the world's largest Pentecostal groups. It is also a member of the Evangelical Alliance.

Courses offered lead to qualifications which include Certificate, Diploma, BA, MA and PhD. These are validated by the University of Sheffield. The College also offers a variety of home study courses.

As part of our commitment to assist in training for Christian service at a wide variety of levels, it has been decided that the essence of some of the courses taught at Mattersey Hall should be made available in book form. Such books will, therefore, normally be authored by the College tutor who teaches the course in question.

As a matter of policy our publications will be written in a highly readable style without lacking academic integrity.

The Holy Spirit - an Introduction has been authored by Dr David Petts and is published in 1998 to celebrate his 21st year as Principal of the College and the 25 years the College has been situated at Mattersey Hall.

Mattersey Hall, Mattersey, DN10 5HD, England.

About the author

Dr David Petts has been Principal of Mattersey Hall since 1977. A former Exhibitioner of Brasenose College, Oxford, his academic achievements include an MA, an MTh, and a PhD in Theology.

An international Bible teacher, he emphasises the work of the Holy Spirit in the Christian's life and has been instrumental in leading many into the experience of the Baptism in the Holy Spirit. He conducts seminars and Bible Studies in churches, colleges and universities.

David is an Assemblies of God minister and much of his ministry has been within the world-wide Pentecostal Movement. He is, however, often to be found preaching in interdenominational gatherings, especially where the congregation are sympathetic to his charismatic emphasis.

He is married to Eileen who has been a strong support to his ministry for some 35 years. Their three children are all married and all involved in local church leadership.

Contents

Preface

Introduction

1 Who is the Holy Spirit?

2 The Spirit before Pentecost - OT

3 The Spirit before Pentecost - NT

Author's Preface

I suppose I experienced the work of the Holy Spirit in my life before I knew a thing about him. That's probably how it is with most people. We learn about the Holy Spirit *after* we become Christians and yet, if it had not been for the Holy Spirit's activity, we would never have become Christians at all.

I know all that now, but as I grew up in a Christian family I did not appreciate that the godly influence of my parents was a result of the Holy Spirit at work in their lives. Neither did I realise that when, at the age of fourteen, I committed my life to Christ and received him as my saviour, it was the Holy Spirit who had been at work in me leading me to repentance and faith.

Of course I had heard about the Holy Spirit. He was mentioned at the close of every service when our Baptist minister pronounced the benediction. And when I was baptised in water shortly after becoming a Christian I was baptised *in the name of the Father, and of the Son and of the Holy Spirit.* I knew that he was the Third Person of the Trinity although I had little idea of what that meant, but apart from that we received very little teaching about him.

And then, at the age of nineteen, while on holiday in Switzerland, I met some Pentecostals. It seemed to me that they had something in their Christian life that was lacking in mine, and when I asked them what it was I was told that, if there was a difference, it was probably the 'Baptism in the Holy Spirit' - something I'd never heard about before, even though the Lord Jesus had told his disciples not to set about the task of world evangelisation without it!

They encouraged me to go away and read the Book of Acts for myself and to let it challenge me. I'm glad that nobody had put into my head the foolish notion, current in some circles, that 'you can't get doctrine from Acts'. (Such people can't have read 2 Timothy 3:16!) All scripture is profitable for doctrine and the Book of Acts certainly spoke clearly to me at that time. As a result, about a year later, just a few weeks before starting my course at Oxford University, after months of searching, I was baptised in the Spirit in a Pentecostal prayer meeting and spoke in a language I had never learned for some forty-five minutes.

That was a major turning point in my life. It was before the days of the charismatic renewal, which in England began in the early sixties, and it was not possible then to remain in one's denomination and maintain a 'Pentecostal' experience, especially if you wanted to seek for and to exercise spiritual gifts. So my fiancee, Eileen, and I left our Baptist churches and joined the Assemblies of God, where we have been happily engaged in fellowship and ministry ever since.

But that does not mean that I'm completely satisfied with the Pentecostals. Some seem all too ready to chase after some new spiritual experience without waiting to evaluate it according to the scriptures. Others are Pentecostal in name only and have never received or have not maintained the charismatic dimension of life in the Spirit which comes with the baptism in the Holy Spirit. What a tragedy that in some 'Pentecostal' churches up to half the people have not yet been baptised in the Spirit!

Perhaps it is here that this book differs slightly in emphasis from the traditional Pentecostal position. Pentecostals usually argue that the Baptism in the Spirit is received *subsequent* to conversion. This is a position which I myself once adopted[1] . I

---

[1] See *The Dynamic Difference,* Springfield MO, GPH, 1978, pp 16-20.

have now come to see, however, that to talk of subsequence is probably unhelpful, for it tends to separate the Baptism too far from conversion. The Baptism in the Spirit is by no means the same as conversion, but it can certainly happen at the same time (as appears to have been the case with Cornelius in Acts 10), and it should certainly be received as soon as possible after conversion. That is why I have referred to it in this book as an 'at/after' experience.

Of course I hope that what I have written will lead to a clear and correct understanding of the person and work of the Holy Spirit. A right understanding of what the Bible teaches is the only sure means of evaluating what comes from the Spirit and what does not. But more especially it is my prayer that, as a result of what is written in these pages, those who are in responsible positions of leadership in local churches, whether 'Pentecostal' or 'Charismatic' or otherwise, may see the urgent necessity of instructing young converts and leading them, early in their Christian experience, into the charismatic dimension of the Baptism in the Holy Spirit.

This is the emphasis we place in our training of future church leaders at Mattersey Hall. In concluding this preface it remains only for me to thank my wife, and all my colleagues who have worked with me in the College over the past 20 years, for all their support and encouragement. The Lord has done great things for us, and he will continue to do so as we seek to train others to serve the Lord Jesus in the power of the Holy Spirit.

David Petts
Mattersey Hall
January 1998.

Introduction

A Wonderful Start

This book is about the Holy Spirit and it's written for Christians. So let me begin by pointing out how important the Holy Spirit is to us as Christians. In fact we would not *be* Christians if it were not for the work of the Spirit in our lives[1] and we certainly have no hope of winning the world for Jesus without the Spirit's power. That's why the Lord Jesus, just before he left his disciples and returned to heaven, gave them strict instructions not to attempt the task of world evangelisation until they had received the power of the Holy Spirit[2].

The Book of Acts[3] gives us a thrilling account of how the young Christian Church, as a result of what happened on the Day of Pentecost[4], was enabled through the dynamic of the Spirit to make a wonderful start in reaching the world for Jesus. The completion of that task is now entrusted to us and if we are to succeed in our mission we must know both in *theory* and in *practice* as much as we possibly can about the person and work of the Holy Spirit.

Experience the Spirit

Of course, it's not enough to know the theory! For centuries the Christian Church made formal acknowledgment of the Holy Spirit in its creeds and in its liturgy, but it was not until the early pentecostals began to emphasize the importance of the miracle-working power of the Spirit for today that the

---

[1] John 3:3-8 makes it clear that the New Birth is the work of the Holy Spirit. More of this later.

[2] Luke 24:49, Acts 1:4, 5-8

[3] The Book of Acts is usually described as *The Acts of the Apostles* though might be better called *The Acts of the Holy Spirit.*

[4] Acts 2:1-4 ff

Church began to rediscover the wonderful potential of letting the Holy Spirit have his way. The phenomenal growth of the Pentecostal Movement in the second half of the twentieth century offers abundant evidence of this[1], but the pentecostals of this generation must take care that their experience of the Spirit is no less than that of their fathers. It is not enough to hold to pentecostal doctrine. We must experience the Spirit's power.

The Test of Genuine Experience

But to emphasize the importance of receiving the Spirit's power is not to say that we must covet spiritual experience to the exclusion of sound doctrine. I understood what the American lady meant when she said to me in a home-group meeting some years ago, 'David, I don't want *doctrine*. I want *God*!' She was tired of the dry deadness of denominational dogma. She longed for the life of the Spirit! But she was really missing an important point. There is a vital link between experience and doctrine. If our spiritual experience today is to be recognised as a genuine work of the Holy Spirit, then we must be able to measure it against the teaching of Scripture. The Spirit who inspired the writing of the Scriptures in the first place will not contradict himself by acting contrary to them today.

I shall never forget hearing early on in my pentecostal experience Donald Gee's illustration[2] of a sailing boat. It is not enough to have a sail. It needs a weighty keel to give it balance. We need not only the wind of the Spirit filling our

---

[1] In 1966 it was estimated that there were some ten million Pentecostals in the world (Menzies, W.W., *Anointed to Serve*, Springfield MO, GPH, 1971, p. 9). Recent estimates suggest several hundred million.

[2] Donald Gee was one of the early pioneers of the Pentecostal Movement and a former distinguished Principal of the Assemblies of God Bible College at Kenley (now based at Mattersey Hall). His writings are still well worth reading today.

sail to drive our boat along, but the balancing keel of sound doctrine to keep the boat upright. A boat without a keel is unbalanced. Without wind in its sail it gets nowhere! There is no real tension between doctrine and experience. They are both vital in our Christian lives. That's why I have tried in this book to strike a right balance between the doctrine of the Spirit and our experience of the Spirit. I have covered a wide range of topics and questions which I trust will not only help you in your understanding of the Holy Spirit but will lead you into a deeper and fuller experience of the Spirit's life and power.

CHAPTER ONE

Who is the Holy Spirit?

Before we begin to consider the work of the Holy Spirit and the wonderful impact he can make in our lives it is important that we understand who he is. As Christians we believe in both the personality and the deity of the Holy Spirit[1]. That is to say we believe that the Holy Spirit is a person and that he is God. In this chapter we will consider why.

A Wonderful Person

Despite the teachings of the Jehovah's Witnesses and others who try to tell us that the Holy Spirit is an impersonal force, the Bible provides plenty of evidence for his personality. This is made very clear in a number of passages which describe the Spirit as engaging in personal activities and as possessing personal attributes. Furthermore in John's Gospel the pronouns used to refer to the Spirit may be understood to indicate personality, and we're told that the Spirit is just like Jesus who is most certainly a person! As we look at each of these areas in turn we will see that the language used simply wouldn't make sense unless the writer intended us to believe in the personality of the Spirit.

---

[1] In Christian theology the Holy Spirit is 'the Third Person of the Trinity, distinct from, but consubstantial, coequal, and coeternal with the Father and the Son, and in the fullest sense God' (Livingstone, E.A. [Ed], *The Concise Oxford Dictionary of the Christian Church*, Oxford, OUP, 1977, p. 245).

Personal Activities

In the Gospel of John and in the Acts of the Apostles there are several passages which reveal that the Spirit engages in personal activity. This is most clear in John chapters 14-16 and in Acts 13. We'll look at each of these briefly in turn.

Notice what Jesus says in John 14:26: *But the Counsellor, the Holy Spirit, whom the Father will send in my name, will* ***teach*** *you all things and* ***remind*** *you of everything I said to you*[1]. Again, speaking about the Holy Spirit in John 15:26 he says: *He will* ***testify*** *about me.* And in John 16:13 the evidence is even more compelling when Jesus says: *When he, the Spirit of Truth, comes he will* ***guide*** *you into all truth. He will not* ***speak*** *on his own; he will* ***speak*** *only what he* ***hears****, and he will* ***tell*** *you what is yet to come.*

These verses make it perfectly clear that the Lord Jesus himself taught his disciples that the Holy Spirit teaches, reminds, testifies, guides, speaks, hears, and tells. It is absurd to suggest that he is not a person! Indeed the Greek word *parakletos* translated here as 'Counsellor' always refers to a person.

But there is further proof in Acts 13:2 where we read that while the leaders of the church at Antioch were worshipping the Lord and fasting, *The Holy Spirit* ***said****, "Set apart for* ***me*** *Barnabas and Saul for the work to which* ***I*** *have* ***called*** *them".* This verse alone offers clear evidence that Luke, the writer of Acts, believed firmly in the personality of the Holy Spirit.

Personal Attributes

Paul teaches us the same truth as he ascribes to the Spirit not only personal activities but personal attributes too. In Romans 8:26 he tells us that *we do not know what we ought to pray,*

---

[1] All quotations are from the NIV unless otherwise stated.

*but the Spirit himself **intercedes** for us with **groans** that words cannot express.* In this verse the Holy Spirit is described not only as praying - a very personal activity - but as praying with intense emotion[1] as he helps us in our weakness.

Another verse which conveys a similar thought is Ephesians 4:30 where Paul, reflecting the language of Isaiah 63:10, tells us not to ***grieve** the Holy Spirit.* And the extent to which the Spirit was grieved when Ananias ***lied to*** him is graphically described for us in Acts 5:1-10!

Finally the Spirit is portrayed as possessing not only emotion but will. Speaking of spiritual gifts Paul tells us in 1 Corinthians 12:11 that the Spirit *gives them to each one just as he **determines**.*

Personal Pronouns

A further evidence of the Spirit's personality is the use of personal pronouns. We have already mentioned Acts 13:2 with regard to the personal activities in which the Spirit engages, but the use of the personal pronoun *me* is also highly significant in this verse: *The Holy Spirit said, "Set apart for **me** ...".*

A rather more technical example is to be found in John 16:13 where Jesus says *When he the Spirit of Truth has come he will guide you into all truth.* To appreciate this point you need to understand that in the Greek language in which the New Testament was written nouns and pronouns were given a gender (just as they are in many languages today - French, German, Spanish etc). For example, the word for 'bread', *artos*, was masculine; the word for 'glory', *doxa,* was feminine; and the word for 'book', *biblion,* was neuter. And every noun

---

[1] The Greek word for 'groan' here is *stenagmos* a word conveying the sense of intense feeling.

in Greek would have one of these genders, masculine, feminine or neuter. Now with regard to the sentence quoted from John 16:13 what is significant is that the Greek word for 'spirit', *pneuma,* is neuter[1]. Strictly speaking, according to the rules of grammar, John should have made the word 'he', *ekeinos,* 'agree' with the word for 'spirit', *pneuma,* by writing *ekeino* (the neuter form of the pronoun). However, he chooses the masculine form, *ekeinos,* and in so doing may well be seeking to emphasise the Spirit's personality[2].

But if all that was a bit complicated, the next point is relatively simple!

Just like Jesus

The final proof that the Spirit is a person must surely be that Jesus promised to send another Counsellor just like himself. In John 14:16 he says:

> *He will give you another Counsellor to be with you for ever - the Spirit of Truth.*

Quite simply, in the Greek language there were two different words for 'another'. One, *allos,* meant 'another of the same kind'. The other, *heteros,* meant 'another of a different kind'. For example, you could go back to a shop to change an article and ask for 'another' one in exchange. You might decide to have one of the same kind or one of a different kind. Either

---

1 The fact that the word *pneuma* is neuter does not deny the personality of the Holy Spirit. It is the **word** *pneuma* that is neuter, not the Spirit himself. The word *artos* (the Greek word for 'bread') is masculine, but that does not mean that bread is male!

2 A similar use of the masculine where the neuter might have been expected is to be found in John 14:26 and 15:26. However, in both these verses the masculine noun *parakletos* is in close proximity and it is possible that the pronoun might have been 'attracted' into the masculine for this reason. Nevertheless the point holds good in 16:13, for *parakletos* is not in the vicinity.

way in English you would ask for 'another' one. But in Greek you would ask for *allos* or *heteros* depending on whether you wanted the same kind or a different kind of article.

Here in John 14:16 Jesus promises his disciples 'another Counsellor' and the word he uses is *allos.* Jesus had been their helper, advisor, counsellor, until then. But he was going away. Yet in his place he promised them another helper, the Holy Spirit, who would be **the same kind**. Nothing but a person - indeed a divine person - could be to the disciples what Jesus had been! The Holy Spirit must be a person, because he's just like Jesus!

But that leads us on to the subject of his deity, which in itself is a proof of his personality.

A Divine Person

Attributes of Deity

There are certain qualities which belong to God alone. No-one else possesses these qualities. If God did not have them he would not be God! For anyone else to possess them would mean that he too was God! These qualities are sometimes called *attributes of Deity* and one way to show that the Holy Spirit is God is to show that he possesses these attributes.

For example, the Bible reveals that God is *Creator* (Genesis 1:1) but also makes clear that the Spirit is Creator (Genesis 1:2, Job 33:4). God is *Omnipotent* (Matthew 19:26, Job 42:2) and so is the Holy Spirit (Luke 1:35-37). Both God and the Spirit are *Omnipresent* (Jeremiah 23:24, cf Psalm 139:7-10) and *Omniscient* (1 John 3:20 cf 1 Corinthians 2:10). And God is *Eternal* (Psalm 90.2) as is also the Holy Spirit (Hebrews 9:14).

These passages which ascribe to the Holy Spirit qualities which belong to God alone are thus powerful evidence of the deity of the Holy Spirit. If the Holy Spirit is the eternal, all-powerful, all-knowing, creator who is everywhere present in the universe, as these verses teach, then he is undoubtedly God. To this can be added something which we have already mentioned. The Holy Spirit is just like Jesus (John 14:16)[1] and Jesus too possesses these divine attributes.[2] But that brings us to the subject of the Trinity.

The Trinity

As Christians we believe in one true and living God who is revealed in three persons, Father, Son, and Holy Spirit. This belief is known as the doctrine of the Trinity. Those who have not fully understood what Christians believe in this respect have claimed that we believe in three gods. (This was in fact one of Mohammed's main criticisms of Christianity, though he mistakenly believed that Christians taught that the virgin Mary was one of the Trinity!) The Bible, however, does not teach that there are three gods, but that there is *one* God revealed in *three* persons.

It is, of course, extremely difficult for our minds to understand this, but we do well to remember that with our limited intelligence we cannot expect fully to understand the infinite God. If my little mind could comprehend him he would hardly be God! I believe in the doctrine of the Trinity, not because I can understand it, but because the evidence of Scripture demands it. Consider the following verses where the Spirit is *distinct from* the Father and the Son and yet is mentioned *along with* them on each occasion:

---

[1] See my comments on the use of *allos* on p. 10.

[2] For evidence of the deity of the Lord Jesus Christ, see Petts, D., *You'd Better Believe It!,* Mattersey Hall, 1991, pp. 18-21.

He saw the ***Spirit of God*** (the Holy Spirit) *descending like a dove and lighting upon* ***him*** (Jesus, God the Son) *and a* ***voice from heaven*** (God the Father's) *said, This is my Son* (Matthew 3:16-17).

Therefore go and make disciples of all nations baptizing them in the name of the ***Father*** *and of the* ***Son*** *and of the* ***Holy Spirit*** (Matthew 28:19).

I (God the Son) *will ask the* ***Father*** *and he will give you* ***another counsellor*** (the Holy Spirit) (John 14:16).

Exalted to the right hand of God, ***he*** (Jesus, God the Son) *has received from the* ***Father*** *the promised* ***Holy Spirit*** (Acts 2:33).

God (the Father) *anointed* ***Jesus of Nazareth*** (God the Son) *with* ***the Holy Spirit*** (Acts 10:38).

The grace of the ***Lord Jesus Christ*** (God the Son), *and the love of* ***God*** (the Father), *and the fellowship of the* ***Holy Spirit*** *be with you all* (2 Corinthians 13:14).

Christ (God the Son) *who through the eternal* ***Spirit*** *offered himself unblemished to* ***God*** (the Father) (Hebrews 9:14).

Although none of these verses taken alone proves beyond doubt the deity of the Holy Spirit, taken together, and along with other Bible passages, they bear powerful testimony to the view that New Testament writers understood the Holy Spirit to be God.

Other Significant Passages

Two other significant passages which indicate the deity of the Spirit are Luke 1:26-38 and Acts 5:3-5[1]. In the first of these the angel Gabriel appears to the virgin Mary and announces that she will give birth to a son who will be called the Son of the Most High. *How will this be?* asks Mary, *since I am a virgin* (v34). The angel replies:

> *The **Holy Spirit** will come upon you and the power of the Most High will overshadow you. So the holy one to be born will be called the Son of God ....For nothing is impossible with **God*** (vv 35-37).

And the passage in Acts 5 is clearer still. Ananias and Sapphira sold a piece of property and pretended to give the entire proceeds to the apostles. However, they secretly kept back part of the money for themselves. Peter clearly had a revelation from God about this and accused Ananias of lying:

> *How is it that Satan has so filled your heart that you have **lied to the Holy Spirit**...? .....You have not **lied to men but to God!*** (vv 3-5)

This passage, in which Peter equates lying to the Spirit with lying to God, is thus one of the strongest proofs in the New Testament for the deity of the Holy Spirit. Taken along with the other passages we have considered and with the references which ascribe divine attributes to the Spirit it is easy to understand how orthodox Christians down through the centuries have recognised that the Holy Spirit is none other than God himself. But if that is the case, should we not worship the Holy Spirit?

---

[1] Another interesting passage is Acts 28:25-26 where Paul quotes Isaiah 6 and says *The Holy Spirit said....* whereas in Isaiah 6 it is *God* who speaks.

Should we worship the Holy Spirit?

At first sight the obvious answer to this question is *Yes!* There is a long tradition in the church that the Holy Spirit should 'with the Father and Son together be worshipped and glorified' and this is reflected in the Anglican liturgy:

> *Glory be to the Father, and to the Son, and to the Holy Ghost, who was in the beginning, is now and ever shall be, world without end, Amen.*

And in recent years, in keeping with the same tradition, some Christians have been singing:

> *Father we adore you...... Jesus we adore you...... Spirit we adore you* etc

while others have kept quiet in the last verse, unsure as to whether we should worship the Spirit - or else quite certain that we should not!

This, I believe, is partly because there appears to be no New Testament example of Christians worshipping the Spirit and no explicit command to do so. Yet both Old and New Testaments exhort us to worship God, and as we have seen, the Holy Spirit is God. Indeed, to refuse to worship him might well be seen as to some extent a denial of his deity.

But the uneasiness about worshipping the Spirit also springs from a verse of Scripture. In the old Authorised Version, John 16:13 reads:

> *He* (the Spirit) *shall not speak of himself.*

However, the Greek here does not mean that the Holy Spirit would never speak *about* himself - he plainly does on the pages of Scripture! - but that, as the NIV rightly translates it, he would not *speak on his own.* There is no suggestion here that the Spirit ought not to be worshipped. Indeed Jesus uses the same expression of *himself* in John 5:19 when he says that he can do nothing *by himself.* And Christians find little difficulty in worshipping Jesus! The verses in question simply imply that neither Jesus nor the Holy Spirit work in an independent manner, but always in perfect harmony with God the Father and each other. So whatever we believe about worshipping the Spirit, we should certainly not base it on John 16:13.

In conclusion, then, although there appears to be no scriptural precedent or exhortation for Christians to worship the Spirit, we cannot say that there are no scriptural *grounds,* for since the Spirit is God we may well feel it appropriate to worship him. Perhaps we should not discourage people from worshipping the Spirit (along with the Father and the Son, of course), but neither should we emphasise such a practice in the light of the lack of a biblical precedent[1].

---

[1] Closely connected with the idea of worshipping the Spirit is that of talking or praying to him. To suggest that *the fellowship of the Holy Spirit* (2 Corinthians 13:14) implies talking to the Spirit in terms of having fellowship with him is probably to strain the context in which the phrase is set. However, I can find no fault with the argument that we are to listen to and talk to the Spirit on the grounds that as the Paraclete he is the helper who came to take the place of Jesus when he went away. Compare my comments on the Spirit being 'Just like Jesus' on page 10.

CHAPTER TWO

The Spirit Before Pentecost - OT

The amazing events which took place at Pentecost in the second chapter of Acts were undoubtedly a turning point in human history. Before Pentecost the Spirit had been given to a relatively small number of people in order that they might fulfill some specific task to which the Lord had called them. At Pentecost the apostle Peter declared that Joel's prophecy that the Spirit would one day be poured out on all people had now been fulfilled[1] and from that day forward the promise of the Spirit was available to all who would repent and be baptized[2].

We shall be considering the significance of this later, but I mention it now simply to explain why in this chapter and the next we'll be looking at the Spirit's work *before* Pentecost before turning to a more detailed examination of his person, work and ministry *after* Pentecost. In this chapter we'll be taking a look at the Old Testament and we'll examine the meaning of the word *spirit* before considering some examples of God's Spirit at work .

The Meaning of 'Spirit'

The word which is usually translated *spirit* in our Old Testament is the Hebrew noun *ruach.* It occurs 378 times and comes from a verb which means *to breathe out violently.* Consequently it usually means either *wind, breath,* or *spirit* depending on the context. When it is used to mean *spirit* it

---

[1] Compare Joel 2:28-32 with Acts 2:17-21

[2] Acts 2:38-39

can refer to the Spirit of God, the spirit of man[1], or an evil spirit[2]. An interesting example of a passage where the word is used with all three meanings (*wind, breath*, or *spirit*) is the well-known story of Ezekiel's valley of dry bones (Ezekiel 37:1-14). Here the NIV translates *ruach* as *spirit* (vv1, 14), *wind* (v9), and *breath* (vv5, 6, 8, 9, 10). Yet although it is clear from the passage that the word can carry these three meanings it is not entirely clear whether any great distinction is intended between them. There seems to be an interplay of meaning suggesting that the Spirit of God is the breath of God (more powerful than the wind, for it can give life to the dead), and that this divine breath in man is that which causes him to live.

The Spirit of God

The phrase *Holy Spirit* occurs only three times[3] in the Old Testament but the expression *The Spirit of the Lord* is found much more frequently[4], the word *ruach* being applied to God 136 times . From these references we learn that God's Spirit is the creator and sustainer of the universe, everywhere present in it, renewing it and seeking to transform man morally, and, as he sovereignly chooses, empowering him for service.

In Genesis 1:2 God's Spirit is revealed as moving over the waters at creation and a similar thought is expressed in Psalm 33:6:

---

[1] eg Genesis 26:35, Numbers 5:14, 14:24, Job 20:3, Psalms 32:2, 51:10. Often the state of a man's spirit determines his course of action (Proverbs 16:32, 25:28, Haggai 1:14).

[2] eg 1 Samuel 16:16. Cf 1 Kings 22:19-25 where it seems that a personal spirit is intended

[3] Psalm 51:11, Isaiah 63:10, 11

[4] Our examination of the Spirit's work in the Old Testament will, therefore, extend to any reference to the word *spirit* where the context suggests that it is God's Spirit who is referred to irrespective of the precise title given to him.

By the word of the Lord were the heavens made and all their starry host by the breath (ruach) of his mouth.

According to Psalm 104:30 all living things are dependent on the Spirit for their life for

When you send your Spirit they are created, and you renew the face of the earth.

And we read in Job 33:4 that

The Spirit of God has made me, the breath of the Almighty gives me life.

What's more, there's nowhere man can hide from the presence of the creator Spirit, for in Psalm 139:7-10 David asks:

Where can I go from your Spirit? Where can I flee from your presence? If I go up to the heavens you are there; if I make my bed in the depths, you are there. If I rise on the wings of the dawn, if I settle on the far side of the sea, even there your hand will guide me, your right hand will hold me fast.

It is clear from these verses that, as we saw in the last chapter, the Spirit is none other than God himself. He created the heavens and the earth, the sea and the dry land. He gives life to man and to every living creature on the face of the earth. There is nowhere we can travel that the Spirit of God is not with us. The Spirit is not simply *there.* He is there *to guide us and hold us fast.* He is not just the great creator of the universe, but he's there along side us, ready to help. This leads us naturally on to consider what the Old Testament has to say about the Holy Spirit's relationship with man.

The Spirit in Relation to Man

The Holy Spirit's relationship with man extends far beyond the fact that man's existence on this planet is due to the work of the Spirit of God. Ever since man first sinned and separated himself from God, God's purpose has been to draw man back to himself. It is the New Testament that makes it clear[1] that God does this by his Spirit, but even in the Old Testament there are indications that conviction of sin is a part of the Spirit's work. Genesis 6:3 talks of God's Spirit contending with man in the days of Noah and in Psalm 51:11 the penitent David prays that God will not take his Holy Spirit from him. More important still in this connection is the prophecy of Ezekiel that God would one day cleanse his people, giving them a new heart and putting his Spirit within them (Ezekiel 36:26-27).

Thus the Old Testament foreshadows the teaching of the New Testament revealing that the Spirit's work is not only creation, but re-creation, convicting men of sin and making them anew. But this is by no means all that it teaches with regard to the Spirit's relationship with man, for by far the major emphasis in the Old Testament in this respect is the Spirit's role in equipping and empowering men and women for special tasks of service.

Power for Service

Old Testament writers use a variety of expressions to refer to the Spirit's work in empowering man for service. The Spirit is said to have been *in* Joseph, Joshua and Ezekiel[2], to have *come upon* Othniel, Gideon, Jephthah, Samson, Saul, and David[3], and Bezalel, Joshua, and Micah are said to have been

---

[1] Cf John 16:7-11

[2] Genesis 41:38, Numbers 27:18, Ezekiel 2:2

[3] Judges 3:10, 6:34, 11:29, 14:6, 1 Samuel 10:10, 16:13

filled with the Spirit[1]. But in each case, whatever the terminology used, the underlying meaning is clear. The Spirit supernaturally enables an individual to perform a task in God's service.

Usually the task is related to some kind of leadership role. Pharaoh put Joseph in charge of the whole land of Egypt because he recognised that God's Spirit was in him[2]. When Moses delegated his authority to the seventy elders[3] and to Joshua[4] the Spirit came upon them as he did later upon Saul and David when each of them was appointed king[5]. Similarly, during the period of the judges, we read that several of these leaders were equipped with the Spirit's power.

Different Abilities

Yet the power expressed itself in different ways. In the Book of Judges it is almost entirely associated with **military conquest**. For example, we read that the Spirit of the Lord came upon Othniel so that he became Israel's judge and went to war (Judges 3:10). When the Midianites, Amalekites and other eastern peoples joined forces against Israel and were camped in the valley of Jezreel, the Spirit of the Lord came upon Gideon and he blew a trumpet (Judges 6:33-34), and when the Spirit came upon Jephthah he crossed Gilead and Manasseh and advanced against the Ammonites (Judges 11:29).

But perhaps the best known example of how the Spirit empowered a man in battle is that of Samson who received supernatural strength far beyond the normal capability of the strongest of human beings. When the Spirit of the Lord came

---

[1] Exodus 31:3, Deuteronomy 34:9, Micah 3:8

[2] Genesis 41:37-41

[3] Numbers 11:25

[4] Numbers 27:18

[5] 1 Samuel 10:10, 16:13

upon him in power he tore a lion apart with his bare hands (Judges 14:6), struck down thirty men of Ashkelon and stripped them of their belongings (Judges 14:19), and, when the Philistines advanced against him, he found a fresh jaw-bone of a donkey, grabbed it and struck down a thousand men (Judges 15:14-15).

In other passages the Spirit is seen as imparting **wisdom.** Isaiah describes the Spirit of the Lord as

> *The Spirit of wisdom and understanding, the Spirit of counsel and of power, the Spirit of knowledge and of the fear of the Lord* (Isaiah 11:2)

and it is therefore not surprising that we find examples of how the Spirit imparted these qualities to men. Joshua is said to have been filled with the Spirit of wisdom[1] because Moses had laid his hands upon him. Joseph's wisdom and ability to interpret dreams are attributed to the Spirit[2], and a similar conclusion is drawn with regard to Daniel[3]. Closely connected with this is Bezalel's *skill, ability and knowledge in all kinds of crafts* which is attributed to his being *filled with the Spirit of God*[4].

Finally it is noteworthy that the coming of the Spirit in the Old Testament is often associated with **prophecy**. Saul prophesied when the Spirit came upon him[5] and Micah proclaimed

> *I am filled with power, with the Spirit of the Lord ... to declare to Jacob his transgression* (Micah 3:8).

---

[1] Deuteronomy 34:9
[2] Genesis 41:38
[3] Daniel 5:11
[4] Exodus 31:3
[5] 1 Samuel 10:10

Indeed the New Testament tells us that the Old Testament prophets spoke as they were moved by the Holy Spirit[1]. Another very important passage in this connection is to be found in Numbers 11 where we are told of the seventy elders with whom Moses shared in some measure the burden of leadership. Not only did *they* prophesy when the Spirit rested on them (v25) but so did Eldad and Medad (v26) who had not gone out to the tent of meeting but had remained in the camp. Moses' response to Joshua's protest about this is highly significant for it gives us a clear indication of God's earnest desire that *all* his people should receive his Spirit:

> *I wish that all the Lord's people were prophets and that the Lord would put his Spirit on them* (Numbers 11:29).

God's Spirit for All

But throughout the whole of the Old Testament period Moses' longing that all God's people might receive the Spirit remained unfulfilled. The day for God's Spirit to be poured out upon all mankind had not yet arrived. The Spirit came upon a limited number of people in order to equip them for some special form of service. Some received supernatural strength, others were given wisdom or victory in battle. Others prophesied. As we have seen, these people were usually leaders. The average Israelite had no personal experience of the Spirit's power.

Yet that was to change. By the Spirit the prophets foresaw two glorious events. Isaiah foretold that the Spirit would one day rest upon the Messiah whom God would anoint with his Spirit in order that he might preach good news to the poor, bind up the broken-hearted and proclaim the year of the

---

[1] 2 Peter 1:20

Lord's favour[1]. And Joel predicted that in the last days God would pour out his Spirit on all people[2]. The gift of the Spirit would no longer be restricted to a few select individuals, but Moses' longing would at last be fulfilled. God would pour his Spirit upon all his people, young and old, male and female, rich and poor.

How privileged we should feel to know that we are living in those days! We know from the New Testament that Joel's prophecy was fulfilled on the Day of Pentecost (Acts 2:17) and that now *the promise is to us, and to our children, to all who are far off - for all whom the Lord our God will call* (Acts 2:39). But that's a subject for a later chapter.

---

[1] Isaiah 61:1-2. Cf Isaiah 11:1-3

[2] Joel 2:28

CHAPTER THREE

The Spirit Before Pentecost - NT

In the last chapter we took a look at what the Old Testament has to say about the person and work of the Holy Spirit. We saw that, although in those days the Spirit came upon only a limited number of people, God promised that the day would come when his Spirit would be poured out *on all people*, and that that promise would eventually be fulfilled at Pentecost. As we now turn to consider what the New Testament teaches about the Spirit we must remember that, even in the New Testament, some were used by the Spirit *before* Pentecost and that we should, therefore, probably think of their experience as similar to that of the people upon whom the Spirit came in the Old Testament.

New Testament people who experienced the Spirit before Pentecost include John the Baptist, Elizabeth, Zechariah, Mary, Simeon[1], and of course Jesus. We'll begin by considering the experience of Zechariah, Elizabeth, and John the Baptist.

Zechariah, Elizabeth, & John the Baptist

Zechariah and Elizabeth were an elderly couple who, despite the fact that they were upright in the sight of God, had had no children because Elizabeth was barren (Luke 1:5-7). One day, while Zechariah was on duty serving as a priest, the angel Gabriel appeared to him and announced that Elizabeth would bear a son who would be *filled with the Holy Spirit even from*

---

[1] Space forbids detailed discussion of Simeon (Luke 1:21-32) who knew the moving and revelation of the Spirit because *the Spirit was upon him.*

birth (v15) and who would prepare the people for the coming of the Lord.

When Zechariah questioned this his powers of speech were taken away because of his unbelief. Nevertheless, Elizabeth became pregnant as the angel had predicted and in due time John the Baptist was born. Then Zechariah was enabled to speak again and *was filled with the Holy Spirit and prophesied* (v67).

Meanwhile, Mary had also heard from Gabriel that she too was to have a son and went to visit Elizabeth who was her cousin. As soon as Mary entered the house and greeted Elizabeth *the baby leaped in her womb and Elizabeth was filled with the Holy Spirit* (v41) and spoke out with a loud voice prophetic words of blessing to Mary.

In connection with this whole story three things are highly significant. First, it is noteworthy that all three members of the family are said to have been filled with the Spirit. That was a rare, possibly unprecedented occurrence, but it foreshadowed the day when, after the disciples had been filled with the Spirit, Peter could declare to the new converts at Pentecost

> *.... you will receive the gift of the Holy Spirit. The promise is for you and your children and for all who are far off - for all whom the Lord our God will call (Acts 2:38-39).*

Second, the infilling of the Spirit was expressed vocally and prophetically. John was filled with the Spirit that he might proclaim the coming of the Christ. Elizabeth pronounced words of prophetic blessing upon Mary, and Zechariah both praised God and prophesied. This too may be seen as prophetic of Pentecost when the infilling of the Spirit was expressed both vocally and prophetically as the disciples spoke in languages they had never learned.

Finally, it is significant that, in John's case at least, the infilling of the Spirit was directly connected with turning many to God (Luke 1:15-16). This is the first reference to the Spirit in Luke's gospel and it can hardly be a coincidence that, early in his second volume (The Acts of the Apostles) the Spirit's power is given for the same purpose (Acts 1:8).

Thus, although not identical, there are striking similarities between the experience of the Spirit enjoyed by John the Baptist and his family and the experience of the disciples at and after Pentecost.

Mary - The Virgin Birth

Mary's experience of the Spirit, before Pentecost at least[1], is largely connected with the virgin birth. Both Matthew and Luke teach very clearly that Mary was still a virgin when Jesus was born. Matthew 1:18 clearly states that before Mary and Joseph *came together* Mary was found to be *with child through the Holy Spirit.* The angel of the Lord appeared to Joseph in a dream and told him

> *Do not be afraid to take Mary home as your wife, because what is conceived in her is from the Holy Spirit (v20)*

---

[1] Acts 1:14 indicates that Mary was one of those who obediently awaited the coming of the Spirit. There seems no reason to assume that she was not present at Pentecost and filled with the Spirit along with the other disciples.

and makes clear that this took place to fulfill Isaiah's prophecy that a virgin would be with child (vv22-23)[1]. It is also noteworthy that Joseph *had no union with her until she gave birth* (v25). This not only suggests that Mary remained a virgin until Jesus was born but also implies that she did not remain a virgin afterwards. That she and Joseph lived a normal married life after the birth of Jesus is confirmed by Mark 6:3 where Jesus' brothers and sisters are mentioned and James, Joses, Juda, and Simon are named. These other children were conceived in the normal way, having Mary as their mother and Joseph as their father.

The account in Luke is also extremely clear. The angel Gabriel appears to Mary and declares

> *Do not be afraid, Mary, you have found favour with God. You will be with child and will give birth to a son, and you are to give him the name Jesus. He will be great and will be called the Son of the Most High....(Luke 1:30-32)*

to which Mary replies

> *How will this be, since I am a virgin? (v34).*

Gabriel's reply (vv35-37) is that the Holy Spirit will come upon Mary and the power of the Most High (God) will overshadow[2] her. The holy one to be born will be the Son of God. That we are to understand that the birth was to be

---

[1] Cf Isaiah 7:14. Note that although the Hebrew here may be translated *young woman* rather than *virgin* it is clear from the context in Matthew that he intends us to understand that Mary was a virgin.

[2] This terminology is reminiscent of the pillar of cloud which overshadowed the camp of Israel in the Old Testament and which symbolized the immediate presence of God (Exodus 13:21, Numbers 9:15-23, 10:34).

supernatural is confirmed by the angel's concluding words - *For nothing is impossible with God.*

Finally, if there could still be any doubt that Luke intends us to understand that Jesus was the Son of God and not the son of Joseph, Luke 3:23 surely clinches the matter. Here we are told that Jesus was, *so it was thought,* the son of Joseph. Indeed, when Mary refers, quite naturally, to Joseph as Jesus' father (Luke 2:48), Jesus politely reminds her who his Father really is (v49).

The New Testament clearly teaches, therefore, that Jesus, the Son of God, was conceived by the Holy Spirit and born of the virgin Mary. This is not only completely reasonable, for *with God all things are possible*, but it is also perfectly logical, for how else could Jesus be both *Son of God* and *Son of Man?* He was *born of a woman* (Galatians 4:4), but he is also *the man from heaven* (1 Corinthians 15:47).

Jesus

Yet even though Jesus' birth was the result of the supernatural operation of God the Holy Spirit, this alone was not enough to equip him for the ministry for which God had sent him. Even he needed to receive the Spirit's power.

The Spirit at Jesus' Baptism

All four gospel-writers tell us something about the baptism of Jesus and relate how the Spirit came upon him[1]. We are told that vast crowds of people came to hear John the Baptist preach and to be baptized by him in the River Jordan. His message was that people should repent (Matthew 3:1-12, Mark 1:1-8, Luke 3:1-18, John 1:6-28) and that although he, John, was baptizing with water, someone greater than he was

---

[1] Matthew 3:13-17, Mark 1:9-11, Luke 3:21-22, John 1:29-34

coming - someone who would *baptize with the Holy Spirit*[1] (Matthew 3:11, Mark 1: 8, Luke 3:16, John 1:33). This person would be the one on whom John saw the Spirit come down (John 1:33).

When Jesus came to be baptized by John (Matthew 3:13, Mark 1:9, Luke 3:21), John refused because he felt unworthy (Matthew 3:14). But Jesus insisted, saying that it was appropriate for him to *fulfil all righteousness*. Then John agreed (Matthew 3:15) and Jesus was baptized.

As he came up out of the water (Matthew 3:16, Mark 1:10) Jesus was praying (Luke 3:21)[2]. Then the Spirit of God descended like a dove and rested on him (Matthew 3:16, Mark 1:10, Luke 3:21-22) and a voice from heaven said *This is My Son, whom I love; with him I am well pleased* (Matthew 3:17, Mark 1:11, Luke 3:22).

After this Jesus was led by the Spirit into the desert where he was tempted by the devil (Matthew 4:1, Mark 1:12, Luke 4:1). It was then that his ministry of preaching, teaching, and working miracles began (Luke 4:18ff).

Baptism and the Spirit

Now from the above summary of what the New Testament teaches about the baptism of Jesus it seems clear that there is a relationship between water-baptism and the coming of the Spirit. Notice, first, that in all four gospels being baptized in the Holy Spirit is distinguished from being baptized in water. *John* was baptizing in water but *Jesus* would baptize with the

---

[1] Matthew and Luke add *and fire*. For an excellent discussion of the meaning of this phrase, see Horton, S.M., *What the Bible Says about the Holy Spirit*, Springfield MO, GPH, 1976, pp 84-89).

[2] Luke says that the Spirit came upon Jesus as he was praying. Mark tells us that the Spirit came down as Jesus was coming up out of the water. I therefore conclude that Jesus was praying as he came up out of the water.

Holy Spirit. The nature and purpose of baptism in the Spirit is not made clear here - Jesus himself does that in Acts 1:4-8 - but it is evident that Spirit-baptism is not only distinct from water-baptism but also vastly superior to it and more important than it. Jesus is greater than John, and the Spirit is greater than water! Water-baptism must, therefore, never be confused with Spirit-baptism though it may be seen as both a symbol of it and, in some sense, a preparation for it[1].

Nevertheless, although we must always remember that the baptism in the Spirit is to be clearly distinguished from baptism in water, Jesus' baptism does indicate that there is a close relationship between them. We shall say much more about this later, but it's sufficient to notice here that the Holy Spirit came upon Jesus *at* or at least *immediately after* his baptism in water. We might say that he received the Spirit *'at-after'* baptism.

I have used the phrase *at-after* because it seems to me to express most adequately what the New Testament teaches about the timing of the baptism in the Holy Spirit in relation to water-baptism (here in the case of Jesus, and elsewhere). The need to invent such terminology springs from the fact that, if we say that the baptism in the Spirit occurs *at* baptism we are in danger of identifying it *with* baptism. On the other hand, if we say that it occurs *after* baptism we are in danger of removing it too far from baptism. The fact is that in the New Testament the baptism in the Spirit generally occurred *at about the same time as* baptism in water. It happened so close to it that we might reasonably say that it happened *at* baptism. Yet its timing was usually sufficiently distinct from baptism for us truthfully to say that it happened *after* baptism. That is why I have invented the expression *at-after.*

---

[1] As we shall see in a later chapter, in Acts water baptism usually precedes Spirit-baptism. The only exception is the household of Cornelius (Acts 10:44ff).

The baptism of Jesus well illustrates the point I am trying to make. Consider the following literal translations:

> *Jesus, having been baptized, came up immediately from the water; and behold the heavens were opened and he saw the Spirit of God coming down on him like a dove* (Matthew 3:16)
>
> *And Jesus was baptized in the River Jordan by John. And immediately, coming up out of the water, he saw the heavens being torn open and the Spirit coming down like a dove* (Mark 1:9-10)
>
> *And it came to pass that, while all the people were being baptized, Jesus also having been baptized and continuing to pray, heaven was opened and the Holy Spirit descended....* (Luke 3:21-22).

We notice that in Matthew Jesus has already been baptized, but he is hardly out of the water when the Spirit comes upon him. In Mark he is coming up out of the water. In Luke he has been baptized and is continuing to pray when the Spirit descends. From this it is clear that Jesus' reception of the Spirit occurred after his baptism in water and yet is in a very real sense a definite part of it. It will be important to bear this in mind later when we come to consider the baptism in the Holy Spirit in Acts. We must reject the teaching of those who argue that the Spirit is automatically received at baptism, for reception of the Spirit is distinct from baptism. Yet we must equally strongly resist the temptation to make a wide separation between them, for they are closely associated in the New Testament. We should expect people to receive the baptism in the Holy Spirit at or shortly after water-baptism (unless, like Cornelius, they have already received beforehand). For the promise still holds true:

Repent, and be baptized.............. and you will receive the gift of the Holy Spirit..... (Acts 2:38).

The Temptation in the Desert

Matthew, Mark and Luke all tell us that after his baptism Jesus was led *by the Spirit* into the desert where he was tempted by the devil. Indeed Matthew 4:1 clearly indicates that the temptation was the *purpose* of Jesus' being led into the desert. He was led by the Spirit into the desert *to be* tempted by the devil. At first sight this seems a rather surprising statement. The Lord Jesus himself taught us to pray that we should not be led into temptation and James 1:13 makes it clear that no-one is tempted *by* God. So why did the Spirit lead Jesus to be tempted?

Before attempting to answer this question we need to remember that although God tempts nobody he may nevertheless sometimes *allow* temptation in order that we might be tested. Paul tells us in 1 Corinthians 10:13 that God will not allow us to be tempted more than we can bear and that he will always provide a way of escape. In Jesus' case God knew that he was able to fight off the devil's temptations successfully[1]. But what was God's *purpose* in allowing his temptation? This may be summarised as follows:

So that Jesus might truly sympathise with us in our temptations

In Hebrews 4:15 we are told that Jesus is a high priest who can sympathise with our weaknesses because he was tempted in every way just as we are - yet was without sin.

---

[1] In my view this does not mean that Jesus *could* not have sinned, as some have taught. If that were the case Jesus would not have realistically been tempted *in every way just as we are* and could not truly *sympathise with our weaknesses* (Hebrews 4:15).

So that he might succeed where Adam failed

In several passages Paul contrasts Jesus with Adam and refers to him as *the last Adam*[1]. The temptations Christ resisted in the desert may be compared with the original temptation faced by Adam in the garden of Eden (Genesis 3).

So that he might demonstrate his perfection

Hebrews 9:14 tells us that *through the eternal Spirit* Christ *offered himself unblemished to God.* Nothing but a perfect sacrifice could atone for sin. In overcoming the temptations to which all other human beings have succumbed Jesus demonstrated that he was a worthy sacrifice for the sins of the whole world.

So that we might learn from his example how to deal with temptation

Because Jesus has overcome temptation he has shown us how it is possible for us to do so. In this connection notice the importance of keeping *full of the Spirit,* of being *led by the Spirit* (Luke 4:1)[2], and of correctly understanding and using the *Spirit's sword*, the word of God[3]. Notice, too, that Jesus was tempted to doubt what had happened when the Spirit came upon him after his baptism. God had said, *You are my Son* (Luke 3:22), but Satan came with the temptation, *If you are the Son of God....* (Luke 4:3, 9). As Christians we are sometimes tempted to doubt the genuineness of what

---

[1] Eg Romans 5:12ff, 1 Corinthians 15:12ff (esp. vv45ff)

[2] It is noteworthy that Luke says that Jesus was led by the Spirit *in* (not 'into') the desert. The suggestion is perhaps that the Spirit assisted Jesus during his temptations.

[3] The Word of God is called the *sword of the Spirit* in Ephesians 6:17. Jesus used that sword against the enemy by quoting the Word in connection with each temptation (Matthew 4:4, 7, 10).

happened at our baptism in the Spirit. Like Jesus we must resist with the word of God[1].

So that he might prove that he could be trusted not to abuse miracle-working power

Two of the temptations suggested that Jesus should use his miracle-working power for the wrong reasons[2]. Jesus had received the Spirit in order that his anointed ministry might begin (cf Luke 3:22, 4:18ff). Before embarking upon that ministry it seems that his motivation for working miracles must first be tested.

His Miracle-Working Ministry

Preaching to the household of Cornelius the apostle Peter declared how *God anointed Jesus of Nazareth with the Holy Spirit and power and how he went around doing good and healing all who were under the power of the devil, because God was with him* (Acts 10:38). This verse wonderfully summarises the ministry of the Lord Jesus and confirms the view that Jesus performed his miracles, not by virtue of his deity, but by the power of the Holy Spirit.

Luke records in his gospel how, as Jesus was praying after his baptism[3], *the Holy Spirit descended on him* (Luke 3:22). He says that Jesus returned *full of the Spirit* from the Jordan and was *led by the Spirit* in the desert (Luke 4:1). After the temptation Jesus returned to Galilee *in the power of the Spirit* (Luke 4:14) and in the synagogue at Nazareth Jesus claimed that the Spirit of the Lord was *upon him* (Luke 4:18). These

---

[1] A helpful scripture in this connection is Luke 11:11ff. We sometimes need to remind the devil - and ourselves - that God does not give snakes or stones or scorpions to his children.

[2] ie to satisfy personal desires and to exhibit God's power as a spectacle to the crowds. The right motivation for the working of miracles is love (1 Corinthians 13).

[3] See my comments on page 30 with regard to the timing of this.

different expressions all refer to the Spirit's power and are, as I shall show in a later chapter[1] as we examine the Book of Acts, interchangeable in Luke's terminology[2]. What Luke is telling us here is, quite simply, that Jesus was constantly dependent on the Spirit. The whole of his ministry was in the Spirit's power. Indeed it was by the Spirit that he cast out demons and this, he said, was evidence that the kingdom of God had come[3].

His Death and Resurrection

Finally, before leaving the subject of Jesus and the Spirit, it is noteworthy that it was through the eternal Spirit that Jesus offered himself as a sacrifice at Calvary (Hebrews 9:14), and that by the same Spirit he was raised from the dead (Romans 8:11). Even after his resurrection it was through the Spirit that he gave commandments to the apostles whom he had chosen (Acts 1:2).

The Spirit's work may thus be traced from the moment the Lord Jesus was conceived in the virgin's womb to the day he bade his disciples farewell and returned to his Father in heaven. But the gift of the Spirit was not for Jesus alone. He taught his disciples that they too would receive the Spirit. And that's the subject of our next chapter.

---

[1] See Chapter 6.

[2] This means that we should not understand any essential difference between a person being full of the Spirit, or having the power of the Spirit or having the Spirit upon them. They are simply different ways of saying essentially the same thing.

[3] Matthew 12:28

CHAPTER FOUR

The Spirit in the Teaching of Jesus

In this chapter we shall be considering what Jesus himself taught about the Holy Spirit. His teaching is, of course, found mainly in the four gospels[1] and for convenience we will examine Jesus' teaching on the Spirit in the Synoptic Gospels before turning our attention to the Gospel of John.

The Synoptic Gospels

The writings of Matthew, Mark and Luke introduce us to four main themes about the Spirit in the teaching of Jesus:

1) The Holy Spirit is a gift from the Father (Luke 11:9-13)

2) Miracles performed by the Spirit bear witness to the nearness of the kingdom of God
(Matthew 12:28, cf Acts 1:4-8, Mark 16:16ff)

3) The Spirit helps Christians on trial
(Matthew 10:20, Mark 13:9-11, Luke 12:11-12)

4) The blasphemy against the Holy Spirit
(Matthew 12:24-32, Mark 3:22-30, Luke 11:15-20, 12:10).

Since I shall be dealing with the first two themes in later chapters[2] we will confine ourselves for the time being to consideration of the last two.

---

[1] There is also a brief passage in Acts 1:1-8
[2] See Chapters 6-7

The Spirit helps Christians on Trial

In Matthew 10:19-20 we read the following words spoken by Jesus to his disciples:

When they arrest you, do not worry about what to say or how to say it. At that time you will be given what to say, for it will not be you speaking, but the Spirit of your Father speaking through you.

The accounts in both Mark and Luke are essentially the same. What Jesus is teaching in all these passages is very clear. Christians will at times be persecuted for preaching the gospel. Jesus promises that when we are put on trial we will receive help from the Holy Spirit as to what to say. We need not, therefore, worry about what to say or how to say it.

From these very specific instructions (which will never literally apply to us unless we are put on trial for preaching the gospel) we can learn certain general truths about the Holy Spirit. Christians can expect help from the Holy Spirit particularly with regard to what to say. What's more, the Spirit is able to inspire us to speak spontaneously. This means that we can say the right things despite our own shortcomings or ignorance, or in spite of the fact that we may not have had time to prepare what we should say. Our speaking can in this sense be prophetic because we are enabled to speak what God wants us to speak even if we have no prior knowledge of the subject or the situation.

This does not mean, however, that there is no place for serious study on the part of the Christian worker. It does not mean that the preacher has no need to give thought or preparation to his message. Jesus is not talking here about preparing sermons! He is talking about Christians on trial for their faith, which is of course an entirely different situation. Nevertheless there are times, even in a preaching situation, when the message has been thoroughly prepared, as of course it should be, when the speaker is led to say things he had never before thought of saying. The preaching has at this point become prophetic, and this should not be surprising, for the same Holy Spirit who helps Christians when on trial for their faith inspires preachers when they declare God's word.

The Blasphemy against the Holy Spirit

Because of its very serious nature this subject has been a cause of difficulty for many people. Jesus said that *the blasphemy against the Spirit will not be forgiven..... either in this age or in the age to come* (Matthew 12:32 - cf Mark 3:29, Luke 12:10). Clearly, if blasphemy against the Holy Spirit is the unforgivable sin, then it is vital that we understand what it is.

Here we are faced with an immediate problem. As we look at the passages where this sin is mentioned we discover that, although Jesus warns of its great seriousness, he at no point tells us precisely what it is. However, an examination of the context in which Jesus was speaking should at least give us some indication.

In the account in Matthew 12 Jesus had just healed a demon-possessed man who had been both blind and dumb (v22). As a result of this miracle performed by the power of the Spirit[1] the people were wondering if Jesus might be the Messiah (v23), but the Pharisees denied this and accused Jesus of performing his miracles by the power of Satan (v24)[2]. They were thus attributing to Satan miracles that had been performed by the Spirit's power and it was in response to this that Jesus gave his serious warning about the danger of blaspheming against the Holy Spirit.

---

[1] Cf verse 28

[2] Beelzebub, the prince of demons, is another name for Satan.

But does this mean that the blasphemy against the Spirit, the unforgivable sin, is simply to attribute to Satan a miracle that has been performed by the power of the Spirit? Almost certainly not. None of the accounts tells us that the Pharisees actually committed the unforgivable sin. Jesus was probably warning them that they were *in danger of moving towards it.* This is backed up by the fact that elsewhere in the New Testament, particularly in John's writings, it is clear that what is unforgivable is refusal to believe in Jesus as saviour[1], and, as we shall see later[2], a major part of the Spirit's work is to convict of sin and convert the sinner.

The best way to interpret the blasphemy against the Spirit, therefore, is to understand Jesus as warning the hard-hearted Pharisees (who refused to see his miracles as a sign of his Messianic role and preferred to believe that they originated in Satan rather than admit that Jesus was the Christ) that if they continued along that line of thought they would finally reject all the gracious promptings of the Holy Spirit in their lives and so commit the unforgivable sin of refusing the forgiveness which is freely available in Christ alone.

In the light of all this, how can we best advise those who feel that they have committed the unforgivable sin? We must assure them that the very fact they are at all concerned about it is a sure guarantee that they have not! We must point them to the merits of the blood of Jesus shed for sin at Calvary. There he paid the price and took the punishment for all the sins of all mankind. There is no sin so big that he will not forgive it if we come to him in repentance trusting in his atoning blood. The only unforgivable sin is to refuse the forgiveness he so freely offers.

---

[1] See, for example, John 3:18, 36.

[2] See Chapter 5.

The Gospel of John

We now turn our attention to John's Gospel. We'll concentrate on Jesus' teaching about the Spirit as Paraclete in chapters 14-16 and the interesting passage in John 20:19-23 where Jesus breathed on his disciples and said *Receive the Holy Spirit.* There are of course a number of other references to the Spirit in John's Gospel[1] but these are referred to elsewhere[2].

The Holy Spirit as the Paraclete

Jesus' teaching about the Paraclete is to be found in John chapters 14-16 where we are told some of the things which Jesus shared with his disciples in those last few days just before he was crucified. He made it plain that he was about to go back to the Father (14:12) but that the Father would give them *another Counsellor* (14:16, NIV) who would be with them for ever[3].

The Meaning of Paraclete

The word which the NIV translates as a 'counsellor' here is *parakletos* in the original Greek and from it the word 'Paraclete' has come into the English language. Since it is not widely understood, however, some explanation is necessary. The problem is that no one English word adequately expresses the meaning of the Greek word *parakletos.* A glance at various English versions quickly reveals several of its possible meanings - *Comforter* (KJV), *Advocate* (Weymouth, Rieu, NEB), *Counsellor* (RSV, NIV), *Helper* (Moffatt, NAS, GNB), *Someone to stand by you* (JB Phillips). The Amplified Bible combines them all by saying *Comforter (Counselor, Helper, Intercessor, Advocate, Strengthener, and Standby).*

---

[1] John 1:32-33, 3:5-8, 34, 4:23-24(?), 6:63, 7:39

[2] We have already talked about John 1:33, for example, when speaking of Jesus' baptism in the Spirit

[3] John 14:26 identifies the Paraclete as *the Holy Spirit* - cf 14:17, 15:26, 16:13 where he is referred to as *The Spirit of Truth.*

Since no one English word is sufficient I shall simply use the word *Paraclete*. As we use it we need to bear in mind that it carries to some extent all the meanings referred to above. However its basic meaning is *One who is called alongside to help*. For this reason, if we're looking for a single word to translate *Parakletos*, then perhaps *Helper* is to be preferred, although this has the disadvantage of having possible overtones of inferiority[1]. Furthermore, we must bear in mind that the meaning of the word as used in John 14-16 is best determined by examining how it is used in that context.

The Paraclete and the Christian

Shortly after introducing the subject of the Paraclete (John 14:16) Jesus made the statement, *I will not leave you as orphans, I will come to you* (14:18). To help us understand this we need to know that in those days the disciples of a teacher were often described as his children[2] and so when he died they saw themselves as orphans[3]. In making this statement, therefore, Jesus was promising that after his death the disciples would not be without a teacher. He would come to them in the person of the Holy Spirit so that they might continue to be taught the truth.

This thinking underlies most of Jesus' teaching with regard to the Paraclete in relation to the Christian. The Paraclete came (1) to take the place of Jesus who was going away, and (2) to reveal the truth to Jesus' disciples. Several verses in these

---

[1] For a helpful discussion of the strengths and weaknesses of the various translations of *parakletos*, see:
Carson, DA, *The Gospel According to John,* Leicester, IVP, 1991, pp. 499-500.

[2] Cf Galatians 4:19, 1 John 2:1, 3:18

[3] Rea draws attention to the fact that Socrates' friends considered themselves to be orphans when he died. See:
Rea, J, *The Holy Spirit in the Bible,* London, Marshall Pickering, 1992, p. 155

chapters emphasise these two facts. It was actually good for the disciples that Jesus should go away because if Jesus had not gone away the Paraclete would not have come (16:7), but the Paraclete would be with Jesus' disciples *for ever* (14:16). Jesus himself would not be with them for ever but the Paraclete, who is just the same kind of person Jesus is[1], would come to take his place.

Hitherto Jesus had been their teacher. Now the Paraclete, whom the Father would send in Jesus' name, would teach them all things and remind them of what Jesus himself had told them (14:26). He would guide them into all the truth, would bring glory to Jesus, show them things to come, and make known the things of Christ to them (16:13-15). Jesus had described himself as *the truth* (14:6) but the Paraclete was the *Spirit of truth* who had come to take his place (14:17, 15:26, 16:13).

The Paraclete and the World

And the Paraclete's coming was not just for the benefit of the disciples. Just as Jesus had come into the world that the world through him might be saved, now the Holy Spirit was coming to convict the world of sin and convince[2] of the need of a saviour. In John 16:8-11 Jesus told his disciples that the Spirit would convict the world of sin, of righteousness, and of judgment - of sin, because men do not believe in him, of righteousness because Jesus was returning to the Father, and of judgment 'because the prince of this world now stands condemned'.

---

[1] Such is the force of the Greek word *allos* here translated 'another' as I pointed out in Chapter 1. See p 10. Note also the force of *I will come to you* in 14:18. Elsewhere Jesus promised that he would one day return personally but this verse is not a promise of the second coming. It is a statement that he would come in the person of the Holy Spirit.

[2] The Greek verb used in this passage *(elegcho)* means both *convince* and *convict.* Cf page 53.

The suggestion here is that because unbelief is the root cause of sin[1] the unbelieving world must be convicted of its sin. The Spirit would also convict the world of righteousness because Jesus was going away to the Father. Until that point, he, Jesus, had brought conviction of righteousness by his sinless life. Now the Holy Spirit would fulfil that role. And the world is to be convicted of judgment too. Satan, the prince of this world, stood condemned by Jesus' victorious death at Calvary[2] . Because he is judged, the world under him is also to be judged.

But the Spirit's work in convicting the world of sin is not unrelated to his work in the believer. There is a connection between the Spirit's coming *to us* and his work convicting the world of sin (John 16:7-8). This happens when, through the sanctifying work of the Spirit in our lives, unbelievers are convicted with regard to righteousness. It also happens through our Spirit-inspired testimony or through signs and wonders performed by the Spirit's power (John 15:26-27). But we'll be dealing with that in greater detail in a later chapter.

The Meaning of John 20:22

In John 20:19-23 we read how the risen Christ appeared to his disciples on the evening of that first Easter Sunday. Showing them his hands and his side, he said,

> *Peace be with you. As the Father has sent me, I am sending you.*

---

[1] See Genesis 3:1-4, cf Romans 14:23

[2] Colossians 2:15, Hebrews 2:14, Revelation 12:10-12

Then he breathed[1] and said,

> *Receive the Holy Spirit. If you forgive anyone's sins, they are forgiven; if you do not forgive them they are not forgiven.*

There has been much discussion and disagreement about the meaning of this passage. The argument centres around what precisely happened when Jesus breathed and said *Receive the Holy Spirit.* The obvious difficulty is this. If this was an impartation of the Holy Spirit, how does it relate to the coming of the Spirit at Pentecost? It will not be possible here to deal in detail with the great variety of explanations that have been offered but a brief summary may prove helpful. Broadly speaking theories fall into four main categories and I shall deal with each of these in turn.

John's Pentecost?

Some have suggested that the passage is John's version of the Day of Pentecost. However we need spend little time here for this is hardly an option for those who take seriously the authority of scripture! Acts makes it clear that John was himself present at Pentecost (Acts 1:13, cf 2:14). He heard the rushing mighty wind and saw the tongues of fire! He was himself filled with the Spirit and spoke in other languages as the Spirit gave him the power to do so. He would certainly not have forgotten such an overwhelming experience of the Spirit's power! Neither would he have confused an event which took place on Easter Day with another seven weeks later. Whatever he intends us to understand by this passage he does not intend it as a substitute for Pentecost.

---

[1] The Greek text does not say *on them.* For justification for this translation see Carson, D.A., *The Gospel According to John,* Leicester, IVP, 1991, pp 651-652.

The Power but not the Person

Others have pointed out that the Greek text of John 20:22, *labete pneuma hagion,* when literally translated reads *Receive Holy Spirit.* In other words the definite article, *the,* is missing. They have suggested that this indicates that the disciples received the Spirit's power but not the person of the Holy Spirit himself on this occasion. But does this really help? If this was the Spirit's power, what was Pentecost? And anyway this explanation reads far too much into the Greek. The omission of the article is by no means uncommon in Greek, and as Carson has rightly pointed out[1] Spirit is without the article in the second part of John 7:39 'even though the word clearly refers to the personal Holy Spirit'. In fact *pneuma* is found both with and without the article in this verse and it would be absurd to suggest in the context that the change indicates any shift of emphasis. In short, if all this sounds a bit heavy, this view must be rejected on the grounds that it is based on a misunderstanding of the Greek text.

The New Birth

Another proposed solution is that this was the occasion when the disciples were born again[2]. This is a very attractive explanation for Pentecostals because it offers a model for a two-fold reception of the Spirit. Christians are born of the Spirit at regeneration and are baptized in the Spirit when they are endued with power for service. But although in my view this is undoubtedly true (as I shall argue in a later chapter) this is no good reason for believing that the disciples were born again on this occasion. We must not read this into the passage just because it would suit our theology! The passage does not say that the disciples were born again on this occasion and if Thomas, who was absent could be born again simply by believing, then why did the others need to be

[1] op. cit., p. 650

[2] This seems to be Horton's position. See Horton, S.M., *What the Bible says about the Holy Spirit,* Springfield, GPH, 1976, pp. 127-133

breathed on? A further objection to this view is that *Receive the Spirit* is elsewhere used in the New Testament to refer to the Baptism in the Holy Spirit.

Finally, John Rea rejects the suggestion that this was the occasion of the disciples' regeneration on the grounds that they had already been born again, and claims that it was rather the moment when the disciples became partakers of the resurrection life of Christ and were welded into a new spiritual community, the church[1]. It is difficult to see, however, how such an experience may be understood to differ from the new birth.

A Prophetic Symbol

Finally Jesus' action may be seen as a prophetic symbol[2]. Prophets sometimes acted out their prophecy before it came to pass[3] and the breath of the risen Christ along with the command to receive the Spirit may well have been prophetic of the sound of a mighty wind that filled the upper room on the Day of Pentecost. This is much to be preferred in my view for several reasons.

There is no statement in John 20:22 that the disciples actually did receive the Spirit at this time and there is much to suggest that they did not. There is no record of any marked change in their behaviour as a result of this event as there was later at Pentecost. Furthermore, according to John 7:39 the Spirit

---

[1] Rea, John, *The Holy Spirit in the Bible,* London, Marshall Pickering, 1990, pp. 159-164.

[2] This is Carson's view. He deals with the objection that surely something
must have happened when the risen Christ breathed on his disciples, by pointing out that there is no evidence that he breathed *on* them at all. See note 3 on p. 44. See also Pawson, J.D., *The Normal Christian Birth,* London, Hodder and Stoughton, 1989, pp. 129ff.

[3] See, for example, Ezekiel 4, Acts 21:10ff.

was not to be given until Jesus was glorified and the Spirit was not to come until Jesus went away (John 16:7).

This understanding is also in harmony with the evangelistic context implicit in Jesus' statement concerning the forgiveness of sins. Understood this way John 20:19-23 is parallel to such passages as Luke 24: 45-49 and Acts 1:4-8 in which Jesus promises the Spirit that the disciples might preach the gospel through which alone man might receive the forgiveness of sins.

Thus it is surely not too much to suggest that when the Spirit came at Pentecost with the sound of a rushing wind the disciples recognised his arrival as the breath of the risen Christ, now ascended to the right hand of the Father, breathing upon them from heaven itself! Now was the time that they could *Receive the Holy Spirit* as Jesus had commanded them in that upper room seven weeks earlier. Pentecost was the fulfilment. John 20:22 was the prophetic symbol.

CHAPTER FIVE

The Spirit in the Believer

In the last chapter we considered the teaching of Jesus with regard to the Holy Spirit. We now turn our attention to what the New Testament as a whole has to say about the Spirit's work in our lives as Christians. We'll look first at how the Holy Spirit is at work in bringing men and women to Christ. Then we'll discuss related topics such as his role in sanctification, the fruit of the Spirit etc. We'll leave the baptism and gifts of the Spirit to later chapters because there is so much to say about them, but in doing so, of course, we should realise that they too are a part of the Spirit's work in the believer[1].

The Spirit in the Work of Conversion

Right at the start of this book I pointed out that we would not be Christians at all if it were not for the work of the Spirit in our lives. John 3:5 and Titus 3:5 indicate that we are born again as a result of the Spirit's work and the purpose of the first part of this chapter is to consider precisely how the Spirit brings a person to 'new birth'[2]. We'll see that he does so through the inspiration of the scriptures, the empowering of preachers, and the convincing and convicting of sinners.

---

[1] Another reason for leaving the baptism and gifts of the Spirit until later is that we need to realise that even Christians who have not been baptised in the Spirit do have an experience of the Spirit in their lives. The aspects of the Spirit's work covered in this chapter are those which, in my view, are part of the experience of every born-again Christian, whether baptised in the Spirit or not.

[2] The new birth, or being born again, is sometimes referred to as *regeneration.*

The Spirit inspired the Scriptures

When Nicodemus came to Jesus by night Jesus taught him that if anyone wants to see the kingdom of God he must be born again. This, Jesus made plain, is a work of the Spirit (John 3:5). The same truth is emphasised by the apostle Paul when he says:

> *He saved us through the washing of rebirth and renewal by the Holy Spirit* (Titus 3:5).

On the basis of these verses we sometimes say that the Holy Spirit is the *agent* in regeneration - that is to say he is the person at work in causing us to be born again. However, other Bible verses make it clear that, if the Spirit is the *agent* in regeneration, the Word of God is the *instrument* he uses to bring that regeneration about. 1 Peter 1:23 tells us that we have been

> *born again, not of perishable seed, but of imperishable, through the living and enduring word of God*

and James 1:18 reveals that

> *He chose to give us birth through the word of truth.*

Yet the very scriptures which the Spirit uses in the work of regeneration were inspired by the Spirit in the first place. 2 Peter 1:20 tells us that

> *no prophecy of Scripture came about by the prophet's own interpretation.*

Rather,

> *men spoke from God as they were carried along by the Holy Spirit.*

Similarly, 2 Timothy 3:16 tells us that

> *all Scripture is God-breathed,*

that is, given by inspiration of the Holy Spirit.

Since, therefore, it is through the proclamation of God's Word that we are born again, and since it is the Spirit who inspired the Word to be written in the first place, the Spirit, by the very act of inspiring the writing of the Scriptures took the first step towards our regeneration.

The Spirit inspires the Preacher

But the Spirit does more than that. He not only inspired the writing of God's Word long ago but he continues to inspire and empower those who preach it. In Acts 1:8 Jesus told his disciples that they would receive power when the Spirit came upon them and they would be his witnesses to the ends of the earth. There are many verses which illustrate this truth[1]. Not only do we see the mighty outworking of Jesus' promise throughout the Book of Acts, but Paul frequently refers to the importance of the Spirit's power in his own proclamation of the gospel. In Romans 15:18-19 he speaks of what Christ has accomplished through him in bringing the Gentiles to God

> *by the power of signs and miracles, through the power of the Spirit*

---

[1] See, for example, Acts 4:31, 8:29, 16:6-9, Romans 15:18-19, 1 Corinthians 2:1-4, 1 Thessalonians 1:5, Hebrews 2:3-4.

and in 1 Corinthians 2:4-5 he reminds his readers of how he had first preached the gospel to them:

> *My message and my preaching were not with wise and persuasive words, but with a demonstration of the Spirit's power, so that your faith might not rest on men's wisdom, but on God's power.*

Similarly he reminds the Thessalonians that

> *Our gospel came to you not simply with words, but also with power, with the Holy Spirit, and with deep conviction* (1 Thessalonians 1:5)

and the writer to the Hebrews states that the message of salvation which was first announced by the Lord Jesus himself was confirmed by the apostles who heard him and that God also testified to its truth

> *by signs, wonders, and various miracles, and gifts of the Holy Spirit distributed according to his will* (Hebrews 2:3-4).

It is noteworthy that the major emphasis of these verses which stress how the Spirit empowers the preacher of the gospel is on miraculous signs and wonders. Of course this is not the only way in which the Spirit helps us as we seek to spread the good news, but it is certainly a very important element in it and it is one of the ways in which he convinces and convicts the sinner.

The Spirit convicts the Sinner

In John 16:8 Jesus told his disciples that when the Spirit came he would convict the world of sin. As we saw in the last chapter, *elegcho,* the Greek word used in this passage means both *convince* and *convict.* Traditionally it has been the aspect of *conviction* that has been emphasised[1], and undoubtedly that is part of the meaning of what Jesus was saying, but the *convincing* power of the signs and wonders he performs must also not be neglected.

Perhaps a good illustration of this is the events recorded in Acts 2 with regard to the Day of Pentecost. This helps us very clearly to understand what Jesus meant when he said that when the Spirit came he would convince and convict the world of sin. Notice first that the Spirit *came* (Acts 2:1-4) and that as a result of his coming people from all over the then-known *world* (Acts 2:5)[2] were brought to repentance (Acts 2:37-38). What was the cause of this? Was it because they witnessed the miracle of hearing men speaking languages they had never learned or because of their sense of guilt produced by Peter's Spirit-anointed preaching? Surely the answer is *both.* The convincing power of the miracle made them receptive to the message of the cross (Acts 2:23) which brought conviction of sin[3].

Understood this way, John 16:8, as illustrated by the events at Pentecost, reveals that the Spirit's work is both to *convince* by signs and wonders and to *convict* by the preaching of the cross. In our search for signs and wonders we must not neglect the preaching of the cross. But in our preaching of the cross we must constantly seek the Spirit's affirmation in miracle-working power. To miss out on either would be to neglect a vital aspect of the Spirit's work. It is by both

---

[1] Probably because the *convincing* power of signs and wonders was neglected in the church for a long time. As a result of this, even pentecostals and charismatics have inherited this understanding of John 16:8. But in my view the verse refers as much to his *convincing* work in signs and wonders as it does to the fact that he makes sinners feel guilty.

[2] *Every nation under heaven* is referred to here.

[3] For further evidence that the miraculous can bring conviction of sin, consider Peter's *Go away from me, Lord: I am a sinful man,* after the miraculous catch of fish (Luke 5:8).

convincing and conviction that the Spirit brings sinners to repentance and regeneration.

The Spirit indwells the Regenerate

Once a person has repented and believed the gospel he is then regenerated by the power of the Holy Spirit. He is born again. This has all come about because of the wonderful grace of God, for our salvation is rooted in God's will. It was because of his love for us that Jesus came to die on the cross for our sins. It is by his grace that there is a gospel in which we can believe and be saved. If the Holy Spirit had not convinced and convicted us we would never have come to the point of salvation. But because he did, we were brought to a point of decision, whether or not to repent, whether or not to receive Christ as Saviour.

Understood this way there is no real conflict between the idea of salvation as an act of God's grace and yet as the result of human decision. It is both. God's grace enables me to repent and believe. It does not compel me to do so. But when by his grace I do repent and believe, I am born again through the operation of the Holy Spirit and thereafter know the presence of the Spirit in my heart and life.

Galatians 4:6 indicates that because we are God's sons God has sent the Spirit of his Son into our hearts and Romans 8:9 states plainly that if anyone does not have the Spirit of Christ he does not belong to Christ[1] . It is thus clear that there is a sense in which all born-again Christians have the Holy Spirit, although, as I shall argue later in Chapter Six, not all Christians have 'received the Spirit' in the sense of having received the baptism in the Spirit.

---

[1] The phrase *Spirit of Christ* here is clearly intended to refer to the Holy Spirit as the use of the phrase *Spirit of God* earlier in the verse undoubtedly indicates.

The Spirit in the Work of Sanctification

The subject of sanctification (or holiness) is highly controversial. It has been the cause of great disagreement among Christians in the past and is still the source of much misunderstanding today. Yet the Bible clearly teaches that as Christians we are to be holy for the simple reason that God is holy (1 Peter 1:16) and that he intends us to be partakers of his divine nature (2 Peter 1:4). So it's vitally important that we should understand both *what it means* to be holy and *how* to be holy. In this section we'll be considering both these themes before seeking to show how the Holy Spirit himself is at work in making us holy[1].

The Meaning of Holiness

In the Old Testament the Hebrew word *qadesh* is used in four main ways. Its basic meaning is *to separate* or *to set apart* as when God set the seventh day of the week apart from the other days (Genesis 2:3). But it also carries the idea of *dedication* and *purity* and *usefulness.* Every firstborn male was to be consecrated or *dedicated* to God (Exodus 13:2). The people were to be consecrated and *wash their clothes* (Exodus 19:10)[2] and the priests were to be consecrated in order that they might be *useful* in the Lord's service (Exodus 28:4). Applying these four ideas to us as Christians we understand that when God calls us to be holy he calls us to be separate from sin and from the world, dedicated completely to him, pure and clean so that we might be useful in his service.

With this in mind we can now turn our attention to *how* we become holy.

---

[1] The word *sanctify* is often used in connection with holiness. To *sanctify* means to *make holy*. Another word with basically the same meaning is *consecrate* and this is found frequently in the NIV where AV uses *sanctify*. So *holiness, sanctification* and *consecration* may be viewed as virtually synonymous terms.

[2] Cf 1 Thessalonians 4:7 where holiness is contrasted with uncleanness.

The Means of Holiness

How then can I live a holy life, separate from sin, dedicated to God, and useful in his service? In seeking to answer this question we need to realise first that we're holy **already**. In the New Testament Christians are referred to as 'saints' which literally means *holy ones.* Paul addresses the Corinthians (who were far from perfect Christians) as saints (1 Corinthians 1:2) and reminds them that they had once been thieves and drunkards, but now they were washed, they were sanctified, they were justified in the name of the Lord Jesus and by the Spirit of our God (1 Corinthians 6:11). The tense of the Greek verbs here indicates that their sanctification was something which had already taken place and the context strongly suggests that he is referring to their conversion. When they became Christians they had been sanctified by Christ's death on the cross and were made holy by virtue of their standing *in Christ,* and the New Testament as a whole makes it clear that there is a sense in which Christians are viewed as holy already[1].

Second, we need to recognise that there's a sense in which we're **not yet** holy. To say this is not to contradict what we have just said. The ethical teaching of the New Testament is based on this understanding. It is only because God has made us holy that we can actually *be* holy. So to those who *are* a holy nation (1 Peter 2:9) God still says *Be* holy (1 Peter 1:16). This clearly implies that we're not holy yet and passages such as 1 Thessalonians 5:23-24, 1 Corinthians 1:8-9, Ephesians 5:25-27 and 1 John 3:1-2 all suggest that our holiness will not be complete until the day of the Lord's return[2].

---

[1] See Jude 1, 1 Peter 2:9, Hebrews 10:10.

[2] All this suggests that we have been made holy, we're still being made holy, and we've yet to be made holy. This is completely in line with what the NT teaches on the theme of salvation (of which holiness is a major aspect). We have been saved. We're still being saved, and we've yet to be saved.

Once we realise these things it is easier for us to understand how we may live holy lives. By his death on the cross Christ has done all that was necessary to make us holy[1] and he promises that that holiness will be complete at the Lord's return. These two great facts are the divine incentive which encourage us and enable us to live day by day lives that are well-pleasing in his sight. On the basis of what he *has done* and ultimately *will do* we should strive to be holy *now*. He already sees us as holy because of Christ's cleansing blood. We will one day stand holy before him. In the meantime he calls us to *be* what we *are*.

This is all spelt out quite clearly in Romans 6. We were united with Christ in his death (v5) and must think of ourselves as having died with him (v8). If we count ourselves as dead to sin (v11) we will not need to let it reign in us or to obey its evil desires (v12). In short, it is in the measure that I remember that I am dead to sin that I will in fact be free from sin[2]. That is my responsibility. For his part, God has already made me a new creation in Christ and he continues to cleanse me by the purifying power of his word (Ephesians 5:26, John 17:17). He even chastises me at times so that I might share in his holiness (Hebrews 12:10). But what is the role of the Holy Spirit in all this?

The Role of the Holy Spirit

The question of the Spirit's role in all this is appropriate here not only because this book is about the Holy Spirit, but also because the New Testament does connect the Spirit's work with sanctification (1 Corinthians 6:11, 1 Peter 1:2). It is important to note, however, that these verses are in fact

---

[1] See Ephesians 5:25-26, Hebrews 13:12, Hebrews 10:10, Colossians 1:22.

[2] Elsewhere Paul calls this *putting off the old self* and *putting on the new self* (Ephesians 4:23-24).

referring to the work of the Spirit in regeneration. The New Birth is the only sanctification crisis in the New Testament[1].

In fact the Spirit's role in sanctification is best understood in terms of the fruit of the Spirit to which Paul refers in Galatians 5:22-23. At the New Birth he planted in each believer the seed of the divine nature. As that is fed and watered by the word of God that seed grows and matures into beautiful fruit as the nature of Christ is seen increasingly in our lives. That is the fruit of the Spirit.

The Fruit of the Spirit

In Galatians 5:22 Paul lists nine wonderful qualities which the Holy Spirit seeks to produce in the life of every Christian. *The fruit of the Spirit,* he says, *is love, joy, peace, patience, kindness, goodness, faithfulness, gentleness, and self-control.* These qualities may be seen as a description of the earthly life of the Lord Jesus. We will consider this in the final part of this chapter, but before doing so it will be helpful make some preliminary observations.

Categories of Fruit

In his little book *Fruitful or Barren?* Donald Gee suggested that the fruit of the Spirit could be classified under three headings[2]. Self-control, peace and joy he classified as *fruit for oneself*, patience, kindness and gentleness as *fruit for others*, and goodness, faithfulness and love as *fruit for God*. It needs to be pointed out, however, that this classification is entirely arbitrary, and must by no means be pressed too rigidly. It is

---

[1] We looked at the Spirit's work in conversion in the first part of this chapter. It is *that* work that is referred to in 1 Peter 1:2 and 1 Corinthians 6:11, not some 'second blessing' of 'entire sanctification' as some have taught.

[2] Gee referred to the fruit by the names given in the Authorised Version. In the list which follows I have changed the terminology to come into line with the NIV.

clear that some fruit fall into more than one category - love, faithfulness, and goodness, for example, relate to others as well as to God. Although such a classification may be helpful for preaching purposes it seems highly unlikely that the apostle Paul had any such categories in mind.

Fruit not Gifts

Another important preliminary point is that the *fruit* of the Spirit should not be confused with the *gifts* of the Spirit. We'll be talking about the gifts later[1], but for the time being it will be helpful to note three basic differences. First, the gifts referred to in 1 Corinthians 12, for example, are supernatural abilities imparted by the Spirit for the purpose of building up one's fellow-Christians. The fruit are qualities of character. Second, the gifts are given selectively as the Holy Spirit determines (1 Corinthians 12:11), so that one person may have, say, the gifts of healing whereas another may not (1 Corinthians 12:30). By contrast, the fruit (which is referred to in the singular - *fruit* not *fruits*) is *all* intended to be seen in the life of *every* Christian. Third, it is probably helpful to understand the fruit as springing from the Spirit's regenerative work, whereas, as I shall argue later, the supernatural gifts come as a result of our being baptised in the Holy Spirit[2].

The Fruit in the Life of Jesus

As we read the Gospels it is not difficult to see the qualities of which we are speaking in the life of the Lord Jesus[3]. We'll consider them in reverse order from that which is given us in

---

[1] See Chapter Seven.

[2] This is implied by 1 Corinthians 12:13 where, in the context of spiritual gifts, Paul states that we have been baptised in the Spirit for the benefit of the body (alternative translation).

[3] The examples given are by no means all. A valuable meditation for our private devotions might be to consider the variety of ways in which the fruit of the Spirit are seen in the life of Jesus and how we might learn from them.

the New Testament so that we will conclude with love which is undeniably the greatest of all the fruit of the Spirit[1].

Jesus' amazing *self-control* was manifest in his refusal to turn stones into bread despite the fact that he had been fasting for forty days[2] and in his rejection of the temptation to come down from the cross when taunted by the unbelieving crowds[3]. The Greek word translated as *gentleness* in some modern translations carries with it the thought of *humility* a quality wonderfully exhibited when Jesus washed his disciples' feet[4]. And his *faithfulness* both to God and to his disciples is seen in the Garden of Gethsemane as he finally commits himself to the way of the cross.

His *goodness* was evident for all to see and Peter, when summarising Jesus' ministry, said of him that *he went about doing good*[5]. Similarly his *kindness* overflowed again and again as he met the needs of the poor and needy. Consider, for example, his kindness in turning water into wine at the wedding-feast at Cana in Galilee. We are so often preoccupied with the amazing miracle that we neglect the kindness that motivated it. And his *patience* with his disciples, so slow to learn and to believe, is a model for all who would follow him[6].

Peace of heart, as every Christian knows, springs from that peace with God which results from our being in right relationship with him. Being justified by faith we have peace with God through our Lord Jesus Christ[7]. But Jesus had no

---

[1] See, for example, 1 Corinthians 13:13.

[2] Matthew 4:3-4.

[3] Matthew 27:40.

[4] John 13:1-17.

[5] Acts 10:38.

[6] Even on the eve of his crucifixion they had not truly understood who he was - John 14:9.

[7] Romans 5:1.

need to be justified. He was the sinless one. He always lived in right relationship with Father! And that was the source of his *joy* too. He lived life in God's presence, and in his presence there is fulness of joy[1]. Luke records that Jesus was *full of joy through the Holy Spirit* (Luke 10:21). What a pity that so many stained-glass windows and paintings portray him with a long and gloomy face! Jesus was a man of joy!

Finally, Jesus was a man of *love*. Love is the greatest of the fruit and it is possible to understand Paul's teaching in Galatians as meaning that love *is* the fruit and that the eight other qualities are manifestations of it[2]. Jesus' love is evident throughout the New Testament, not just in the Gospels. Paul could refer to him as the Son of God who *loved* me and gave himself for me[3] and this reference to the cross reminds us that Calvary is the greatest demonstration of love the world has ever seen. The Spirit's work is to make us like Jesus and his highest activity is to pour out the love of God in the human heart[4]. Whatever manifestations of the Spirit we may experience, whatever gifts we may possess, we are nothing if we have not love[5].

Cultivating the Fruit

There is thus no more important pursuit for the Christian than to seek to be more like Jesus, to cultivate the fruit of the Spirit, the highest expression of which is love. The secret seems to be spending time with him. It is as we behold with open face the glory of the Lord that we are changed into his

---

[1] Psalm 16:11.

[2] Compare, for example, Colossians 3:12-14 where love is seen as binding together qualities such as kindness, humility, gentleness and patience.

[3] Galatians 2:20.

[4] Romans 5:5.

[5] 1 Corinthians 13:1ff.

image by the work of the Spirit[1]. One day we shall be like him, for we shall see him as he is[2]!

Finally, before leaving the fruit of the Spirit, we should recognise that Paul sets this list of fruit in stark contrast to *the works of the flesh* which he lists in Galatians 5:19-21. Understood in the overall context in which the letter was written Paul's meaning seems to be that, if Christians revert to attempting to please God by doing the works of the law rather than by trusting in his grace, they will fail completely to do his will. It is only by 'walking in the Spirit' (5:16) that Christians can avoid the works of the flesh. This for Paul means 'crucifying the flesh' (5:24), a theme we considered briefly earlier in this chapter[3]. The fruit of the Spirit will only be manifest in our lives as we seek to allow him to live out Jesus' life through us. In our own strength we can never love as Jesus loved, we cannot even succeed in our attempts to keep his law. It is when we come to the end of ourselves and rely entirely on the power of his indwelling Spirit that we can live lives that are well-pleasing in his sight.

---

[1] 2 Corinthians 3:18

[2] 1 John 3:2.

[3] See pp 56-57.

CHAPTER SIX

The Baptism in the Holy Spirit

As we saw in the last chapter, we would not be Christians at all if it were not for the gracious work of the Holy Spirit in our lives. It was the Spirit who convicted us of sin and who made us a new creation in Christ when we were born again. He implanted within us the seed of the divine nature and that seed grows into beautiful fruit as we allow him to make us more like Jesus day by day.

But that is not the only purpose the Holy Spirit has for us as Christians. He is also given that we might be empowered to be effective witnesses for Christ. Jesus called this being *baptised in the Holy Spirit* and in this chapter we'll be considering what the Baptism in the Spirit is, how it differs from the Spirit's work in regeneration, how we know we've received it. In Chapter 7 we'll talk about how we may receive it if we have not done so already.

Its Nature

Jesus' Last Words

In the first chapter of the Book of Acts we read of Jesus' last conversation with his disciples before he finally left them and ascended into heaven. He gave them clear instructions not to leave Jerusalem until they had received the gift which his Father had promised (v4). This he called being *baptised with the Holy Spirit* (v5) and went on to explain that they would receive power when the Spirit came upon them and that they would be his witnesses not only in Jerusalem and Judea, but to the ends of the earth (v8). The Book of Acts is an inspiring account of how that wonderful promise was fulfilled. It teaches us how the first disciples received the Spirit and, with the Spirit's power, went out to proclaim the Gospel throughout most of the then-known world. By the examples it gives us it teaches us how we may do the same!

The Spirit comes *on* you

One of the first things we learn from Acts is that to be *baptised in the Spirit* is to have the Spirit *come on* you. In Acts 1:5-8 Jesus said to his disciples

> *In a few days you will be* ***baptised with the Holy Spirit....***
>
> *You will receive power when* ***the Holy Spirit comes on*** *you and you will be my witnesses in Jerusalem, and in all Judea and Samaria, and to the ends of the earth.*

From the context it is quite clear that he is referring to the same experience and we may legitimately conclude that the Baptism in the Spirit is the Spirit coming upon a Christian equipping him with power for service. As we read on in Acts we find that the Spirit is said to have come *on*

- the disciples at Pentecost (Acts 2:17)
- the Samaritan converts (Acts 8:15-17)
- the household of Cornelius (Acts 10:44)
- the Ephesians (Acts 19:6)

and it is therefore quite scriptural to consider all these incidents as examples of what it means to be baptised in the Holy Spirit.

However, as we examine these passages we discover that Luke uses a variety of other expressions to refer to the experience of these groups of early disciples and it is helpful to realise at the outset that Luke has more than one way of talking about the Baptism in the Holy Spirit[1].

Interchangeable expressions

If we want to find out what other expressions Luke uses to refer to this experience of the Spirit all we have to do is read through the passages which describe the experience of the four groups listed above. As we do so we discover that he talks about

- being baptised in the Holy Spirit (Acts 1:5, 11:16)
- receiving a promise (Acts 1:4, 2:39)
- receiving a gift (Acts 1:4, 2:38, 8:18, 8:20, 10:45, 11:17)
- receiving power to be witnesses (Acts 1:8)
- receiving the (gift of the) Holy Spirit (Acts 2:38, 8:15, 8:17, 8:19, 10:47, 19:2)
- being filled with the Spirit (Acts 2:4)
- having the Spirit come on, fall on, poured out on, you (Acts 1:8, 2:17, 8:16, 10:44-45, 11:15, 19:6).

Since all these expressions are used to refer to what is clearly the same experience of the Spirit[2], we must understand them to be interchangeable expressions. Yet each expression in its own way sheds extra light on what it means to be baptised in the Spirit. Receiving the baptism in the Spirit is receiving a gift which God has promised in order that we might receive power to be witnesses. To *receive the Spirit* in this way is therefore not the same as our experience of the Spirit's work in our hearts when we are born again, and this can be easily

---

[1] We noticed in Chapter 2 how Old Testament writers also used a variety of expressions to refer to a person's experience of the power of the Spirit. See p 20.

[2] The identity of these experiences is clinched by the repeated use of the concept of the Spirit coming or falling *on* the groups of people in question. Cf p 64.

demonstrated as we consider the purpose, the manner of reception, and the timing of the baptism in the Spirit as compared with regeneration.

Distinct from Regeneration

A Distinct Purpose

Both at the end of his Gospel (Luke 24:49) and at the beginning of Acts (1:4-8) Luke makes it clear that the Father's promise, the Baptism in the Holy Spirit, was to be an enduement with power from on high to enable the Christian in witnessing to the ends of the earth. It was the gateway to the supernatural gifts of the Spirit which both confirmed the gospel message as it was preached (Mark 16:15ff, Hebrews 2:4) and brought edification to the church (1 Corinthians 12:7, 13)[1]. Thus the purpose of the Baptism in the Spirit as described in these passages is totally distinct from the work of the Spirit in regeneration. At regeneration we are 'born' into God's family and become his sons. At the Baptism in the Spirit we are equipped for service. The fact that these two distinct operations may happen simultaneously or very close together (as appears to have been the case with Cornelius) does not mean that they should be identified[2].

A Different Manner of Reception

The Baptism in the Spirit may also be distinguished from regeneration in that it is received in a different way. The Baptism in the Spirit is sometimes received through the laying on of hands (Acts 8:18, 19:6) but there is no suggestion anywhere in the New Testament that the apostles laid hands

---

[1] For the best way to understand 1 Corinthians 12:13, see pp 68ff.

[2] See also my use of the phrase *at-after* in connection with the relation of the Baptism in the Spirit to water baptism. Cf pp 30-32.

on people in order that they might be born again. We are born again when we repent and believe the Gospel.

Furthermore, as we shall see later, in the Book of Acts speaking in tongues was seen as evidence that people had received the Baptism in the Spirit[1]. There is no suggestion that we need to speak in tongues to prove that we are saved!

A Delay in Timing

The timing of the Baptism in the Holy Spirit also distinguishes it from regeneration in that, with the exception of Cornelius and his household, it always appears to have taken place after water baptism[2]. Since the New Testament teaches that water baptism is to be administered to those who had *already* repented (Acts 2:38), believed (Mark 16:16), and become disciples (Matthew 28:19), it follows that the Baptism in the Spirit, since it usually *follows* water baptism, must be a different work of the Spirit from regeneration which according to the New Testament must always *precede* it.

In short, the Baptism in the Spirit is a different work of the Spirit from regeneration. It is an enduement with power from on high. It is usually received after water baptism and often as the result of the laying on of hands. But before turning to the important question: *How may we know that we have received it?* we must answer an objection that is sometimes raised on the basis of 1 Corinthians 12:13.

---

[1] Acts 2:4, 10:46, 19:6

[2] Acts 8:4-25 and Acts 19:1-6 are key passages in this connection. The Samaritans in Acts 8 had already *believed Philip as he preached the good news of the kingdom of God and the name of Jesus Christ* (v12) and had been *baptised into the name of the Lord Jesus* (v16). Despite this *the Holy Spirit had not yet come upon any of them* (v16). It was only when *Peter and John placed their hands on them* that *they received the Holy Spirit* (v17). Similarly the Spirit did not come upon the Ephesians until Paul had laid his hands on them after their water baptism.

The Meaning of 1 Corinthians 12:13

In the NIV the first part of 1 Corinthians 12:13 is translated, *"For we were all baptised by one Spirit into one body"*. On the basis of this verse it is sometimes argued that the understanding that the Baptism in the Spirit is distinct from regeneration must be rejected. The verse is interpreted as meaning that all Christians were 'baptised in the Spirit' when they were born again. This understanding is based on the following reasoning. The phrase *into one body* is seen as identifying the event referred to as regeneration when we become members of the Body of Christ, the Church. The phrase *by one Spirit* is correctly interpreted as *in one Spirit*[1] and the event referred to is thus the baptism in the Spirit. The word *all* is stressed as referring to all Christians. Thus *all* Christians are *baptised in the Spirit* when they come *into the Body* at regeneration. Therefore Baptism in the Spirit is assumed to be synonymous with regeneration and the Pentecostal understanding of Acts deemed to be wrong.

There are, however, a number of problems with this analysis. First, it does not take sufficient account of the context in which the verse is set. Paul is not discussing the Corinthians' conversion, but rather their use of charismatic gifts - especially tongues - within the context of the church. An interpretation which understands the verse within this charismatic context is, therefore, more likely to be correct.

Second, this analysis reads an entirely different understanding into Paul's use of *baptised in the Spirit* from that of Luke. The plain sense of Luke's use of the term is enduement with power for service (cf Acts 1:5 & 8) and it is not just the Pentecostals who have to reconcile Paul's terminology with Luke's! Even allowing for the possibility of differences of emphasis between the two writers, I find it inconceivable that

---

[1] The Greek *en* may be translated as either *by* or *in*.

Luke, as one of Paul's travelling companions, should have such a radically different understanding of what it means to be baptised in the Spirit.

And, finally, there simply is no need to interpret the verse this way. It is possible to interpret the verse in full harmony with the immediate charismatic context of the passage in which it is set, and without reading into Paul's use of the terminology a different understanding from that of Luke. Such an interpretation can only be gained, however, by a fresh translation of the verse.

The problems we have referred to above disappear if we translate the first part of 1 Corinthians 12:13 as follows:

For we have all been baptised in one Spirit ***for*** *(ie for the purpose or benefit of) the one body.*

The essential difference with this translation of the Greek text is the translation of *eis* as 'for' rather than as 'into'. This may be justified on the following grounds.

Although *eis* frequently bears the meaning 'into', this is by no means its only meaning. It also conveys the idea of purpose as, for example, when used with the articular infinitive, and thus may also mean 'for'. The Greek expression *eis polemon,* for example, is used in the context of preparing *for* war and the phrase *eis ti* means 'for what?' or 'why?' A highly significant example of this use is found in Matthew 3:11 where Baptism in the Spirit is contrasted with baptism in water. Here *eis* does not carry the force of 'into', for repentance was required *before* John would baptise, as the preceding verses make clear. Accordingly NIV translates, *I baptise you in water* ***for*** *repentance*. By analogy, the Baptism in the Spirit no more puts a person *into* the body than baptism in water puts them *into* repentance.

More important still, we know that Paul himself understood and used *eis* with this force as is demonstrated by the NIV translation of *eis* as 'for' in Corinthians 8:6 and Ephesians 4:30, and, as I have already suggested, the immediate context of 1 Corinthians 12:13 would not lead us to expect Paul to discuss entrance into the body, but our function or purpose within it. The verse is better understood as reminding the Corinthians that the charismatic gifts they had received as a result of being baptised in the Spirit were not given for their own selfish ends, but for the edifying of others. This underlines what Paul has already said of charismatic gifts in verse 7 - that the manifestation of the Spirit is given to each person *for the common good.* This interpretation is much more in keeping with Paul's overall teaching in chapters 12-14 and on these grounds alone is to be commended.

In short, the simple understanding that *eis* need not mean 'into' dismisses the charge that 1 Corinthians 12:13 contradicts the understanding that the Baptism in the Spirit is a different work of the Spirit from regeneration. When the verse is understood correctly in its context it actually confirms it[1]. The Baptism in the Spirit, then, is an enduement with power from on high. It is usually received after water baptism and often as the result of the laying on of hands. But we must now turn to the important question: *How may we know that we have received it?*

The Initial Evidence

From what we have said so far it is clear that, although all born-again Christians have an experience of the Spirit (for

---

[1] For further discussion of this theme, see my article *Baptism in the Spirit in Pauline Thought* in JEPTA, Vol. 7, No.3, pp. 88-94. See also my article in *Pentecostal Perspectives,* K. Warrington (Ed), Paternoster, 1998, p70ff.

without the Spirit they could not have been born again), not all Christians have 'received the Spirit' in the sense of having been baptised with the Spirit. Since, as we have seen, being *filled with the Spirit* is another expression for being *baptised with the Spirit*, and since we are exhorted in Ephesians 5:18 to be filled with the Spirit, it is clearly of great importance to us as Christians to know whether we have been baptised in the Spirit or not. In this connection it is particularly important that we should hear what the Bible has to say rather than just listening to the testimony of others or relying on our own opinions or feelings. As we shall see, the Bible is extremely clear on the matter.

Evidence is to be expected

In the first chapter of Acts the Lord Jesus himself made it clear that the Baptism in the Holy Spirit is an enduement with power for service[1]. In the second chapter we discover that at Pentecost the Spirit's coming was accompanied by amazing supernatural phenomena - the sound of a violent wind, the appearance of tongues of fire, speaking in tongues[2]. Later on, other manifestations such as prophecy are recorded[3]. Indeed, we can safely say that in Acts the Baptism in the Spirit is always accompanied with miraculous signs[4] and the question naturally arises as to what evidence is to be expected today. How does a person know whether they have received the Baptism in the Spirit or not?

In attempting to answer this question the first thing to notice is that we are definitely right to expect some form of evidence. The idea that we know that we have received the Spirit by

---

1 See Acts 1:5, 8

2 Acts 2:1-4

3 Acts 19:6

4 Even in Acts 8, where no miraculous sign is specifically recorded in connection with the Samaritans' receiving the Spirit, Luke tells us that Simon *saw* that they had received the Spirit (v18).

some 'inner witness' certainly has no basis in the New Testament. Acts makes it quite plain that New Testament Christians were expected to know whether they had 'received the Spirit' or not.

In Acts 2 it is very clear from Luke's description of the events which took place at Pentecost that those first disciples *knew* that they had been filled with the Spirit. Indeed the evidence that a person had been filled with the Spirit[1] was so clear that the apostles could tell the church in Acts 6:3 to choose seven men *known to be* full of the Spirit when they needed to give them the responsibility for the daily distribution of food. The fact that in Acts 8:18 Simon *saw* that through the laying on of the apostles' hands the Holy Spirit was given is further proof that there was *visible* evidence of the Spirit's coming. In Acts 10:44-46 we are told that Peter and his companions knew that the Gentiles had received the Spirit because they heard them speaking in tongues, and in Acts 19:1-7, Paul's very question, *Did you receive the Holy Spirit when you believed?* clearly implies that the Ephesians would have known whether they had received the Spirit or not. In short, Acts makes it abundantly clear that visible evidence is to be expected when a person receives the Spirit. But what evidence may we legitimately consider to be valid?

What Evidence is to be Expected?

To answer this question we must clearly turn to the passages in Acts where Luke describes what happens when people receive the Baptism in the Holy Spirit. These are Acts 2:1-4, 8:14-24, 10:44-48, and 19:1-7. Examining these four passages we discover that three offer us a very full description of what took place. The passage in Acts 8, however, is clearly not a full description in that we are told that Simon *saw* that the

---

[1] Please remember that *being filled with the Spirit, being baptised with the Spirit, receiving the Spirit, etc.*, are interchangeable expressions - see p 65.

Holy Spirit was given to the Samaritans (v18) but we are not told what he saw. The passage itself, therefore, teaches us that it is not a full description. The most we can learn from it is that we should expect visible evidence when people receive the Spirit. But it offers no clear indication as to what that evidence might be and we must therefore turn to the three remaining passages, all of which offer a very full description of events[1].

In his description of the Day of Pentecost Luke records three distinct supernatural phenomena:

> *When the day of Pentecost came they were all together in one place. Suddenly* ***a sound like the blowing of a violent wind*** *came from heaven and filled the whole house where they were sitting. They saw what seemed to be* ***tongues of fire*** *that separated and came to rest on each of them. All of them were filled with the Holy Spirit and began to* ***speak in other tongues*** *as the Spirit enabled them* (Acts 2:1-4).

Of these three supernatural phenomena two took place *before* the disciples were filled with the Spirit. Only one, speaking in tongues, is recorded as a direct result of their having been filled. Further, it is noteworthy that this was the experience of them all. If, as is generally supposed, there were some 120 people present (cf Acts 1:15), then this passage records not one, but 120 baptisms in the Spirit! And the direct and immediate result of each 'baptism' was that the person filled was enabled to speak in tongues.

---

[1] The lack of mention of any specific evidence in Acts 8 is sometimes used to support the argument that we must not be dogmatic about any particular 'initial evidence' of the Baptism in the Spirit. However, since the passage is not a full description, it would be quite wrong to adduce any evidence, positive or negative, with regard to our view of initial evidence. It is simply *not relevant* to the discussion of initial evidence since it neither supports nor denies any particular view.

This in itself is a powerful indication that speaking in tongues is the initial evidence that we should expect to indicate that a person has been filled with the Spirit. This is further confirmed by Peter's interchange with the crowd a few verses later. Amazed by the disciples' ability to speak languages they have not learned, the crowd ask:

> *Are not all these men who are speaking Galileans? Then how is it that each of us hears them in his own native language? .... What does this mean?* (Acts 2:7-12)

to which Peter replies:

> ***This*** *is what was spoken by the prophet Joel, 'In the last days, says God, I will pour out my Spirit on all people.... '* (Acts 2:16-17).

Here it is important to realise that Peter's answer must be understood in the light of the crowd's question. The question was about tongues. It was therefore about tongues that Peter was speaking when he replied when he quoted the prophecy from Joel. The speaking in tongues about which the crowd were asking was the sign that God's promise had been fulfilled. The Spirit was now poured out upon all people.

This brings us to the second of the three passages we are considering - Acts 10:44-48. Here there is no repetition of the manifestations of wind and fire that occurred at Pentecost. Yet Peter and his companions knew that Cornelius and his household had received the Spirit simply because they heard them speak in tongues (v46). Peter refers to this again in the next chapter when he says:

> *As I began to speak, the Holy Spirit came on them as he had come on us at the beginning. Then I remembered what the Lord had said, 'John baptised with water, but you will be baptised with the Holy Spirit'. So if God gave them the same gift as he gave us ...... who was I to think that I could oppose God?* (Acts 11:15-17).

So Peter knew that Cornelius and his household had been baptised in the Spirit because he heard them speak in tongues, just as he and the other disciples had done at Pentecost.

Finally, in Acts 19:1-7, we read how twelve Ephesians received the Spirit. Once Paul had baptised them into the name of the Lord Jesus, he laid his hands on them and the Holy Spirit came on them and they spoke in tongues and prophesied. It is significant that tongues is mentioned first here. The natural way to understand this is simply that it happened first. They spoke in tongues and then they prophesied. Understood this way the passage conforms to the other examples Luke has given us of disciples receiving the Spirit. Speaking in tongues is the first recorded event after people are baptised in the Spirit.

In short, the passages where Luke gives us a full description of people being baptised in the Spirit record some 150 baptisms in the Spirit (120 at Pentecost, a centurion's household in Caesarea, and about 12 in Ephesus). In each case the first recorded event is speaking in tongues. In the light of all this it is clear that Luke intends us to understand that when people are baptised in the Spirit we should expect them to speak in tongues.

Do All Speak in Tongues?

Despite all that we have said so far, the teaching that tongues should always accompany the Baptism in the Spirit is sometimes rejected on the grounds that in 1 Corinthians 12:30 Paul asks the question *Do all speak in tongues?* clearly implying that all do not. As we examine Paul's teaching carefully, however, we discover that he is referring to the use of tongues in church rather than to its use in private.

To appreciate this distinction we need to consider first Paul's teaching in 1 Corinthians 14. Here he indicates that tongues may be used in two quite distinct ways. In verses 18 and 19 he says:

> *I thank God I speak in tongues more than all of you. But in the church I would rather speak five intelligible words to instruct others than ten thousand words in a tongue.*

From this it is clear that Paul spoke in tongues a great deal, yet he did so very little in church. This means that when he spoke in tongues he did so in private and in so doing edified himself (14:4) by praying with his spirit (14:14-15). This private use of tongues is clearly quite separate from its public use in church where, Paul teaches, it must be interpreted so that the church might be edified (14:5, 13, 27-28). The two distinct functions of speaking in tongues, therefore, are first, private, as a form of prayer not requiring interpretation as only God is the hearer, and second, public, as an utterance requiring interpretation since it is heard by the whole church who will not be edified unless it is interpreted.

Now, examining the context of 1 Corinthians 12:29-30, where Paul asks the question *Do all speak in tongues?* it becomes clear that the apostle is referring to the bringing of a public utterance in tongues, for here the gift is coupled with the gift of interpretation - *Do all interpret?* Furthermore, the overall context in which the question is set is that of the believers meeting for public worship[1] and the chapter is a discussion of the function of the different parts within *the body*[2] - in Paul a common symbol for the church.

The question *Do all speak in tongues?*, therefore, when taken correctly in its context, merely implies that not all Christians will speak in tongues publicly. It in no way indicates that they may not do so privately. Indeed, there are very good reasons why they should! As we have already noted, speaking in tongues is a valuable means of edifying oneself spiritually (1 Corinthians 14:4) and is described by Paul as prayer with one's spirit as distinct from prayer with one's mind (14:14-15). Since all Christians have both a mind and a spirit, it is totally inconceivable that God should enable some to pray with their mind *and* their spirit while others pray only with their mind. Clearly, all Christians need to pray with both their mind and their spirit, in their own language *and* in tongues.

The Challenge of Christian Experience

But the most frequent objections are based not on doctrine but on experience. The argument usually runs as follows. Great men of God in previous centuries, as far as we know, did not speak in tongues, and many Christians today claim to have received wonderful experiences of the Spirit, but have never spoken in tongues. Are *we* to say that they have not been baptised in the Spirit, when *they* are sure that they have?

The answer to this is really quite simple. Since the Bible makes it clear that we are expected to know whether a person has been baptised in the Spirit or not[3] it is surely self-evident that there must be some clear recognisable evidence. If we

---

[1] The entire section, Chapters 11-14, is devoted to the correction of disorders in public worship.

[2] Note the frequently repeated use of the term the body in this chapter - 12:12, 13, 14, 15, 16, 17, 18, 19, 20, 22, 24, 25, 27.

[3] See pp. 68-69.

reject the teaching that tongues is that evidence, what is the alternative?

Tongues is the only consistently recurring phenomenon connected with Spirit-baptism in Acts. Once we stray beyond Scripture to some other form of evidence, where does it end? There would be no limit to the strange phenomena that people would claim as evidence of the Baptism! We would be wise to learn what Paul meant when he said to the Corinthians *Do not go beyond what is written*[1]. Precious though the experience of other Christians, past or present, may be, we must never use their experience as a basis for our doctrine.

The Bible alone must always be the basis of what we believe and teach. Our experience is valuable when it illustrates and confirms the message of God's Word. We must not evaluate the Bible by our experience. We must measure our experience against the Bible, and, where our experience is lacking, we must seek to bring it in line with Scripture[2]. In short, if someone tells me he's been baptised in the Spirit but not spoken in tongues, I do not seek to deny his experience. I rather tell him that if he's really been baptised in the Spirit, according to the Bible he could, and should, have spoken in tongues. I encourage him to press on and make up the difference. It requires very little faith to start speaking in tongues.

---

[1] 1 Corinthians 4:6.

[2] That does not mean, of course, that all experiences of the Spirit today will have a precise model in the Bible. God is a God of infinite variety. It is not uncommon, for example, for people to fall down under the power of the Spirit (for which, in my view, there is no precise biblical example). But because such experiences of the Spirit are not recorded in Scripture we should certainly not make a doctrine out of them or teach people to expect them. But neither should we denounce them. We must measure each person's experience against Scripture. The acid test is not whether they have fallen over or not, but whether a change has taken place that brings glory to God and confirms the truth of his Word.

CHAPTER SEVEN

Receiving the Spirit

The importance of receiving the Spirit is stressed by the fact that as soon as Paul reached Ephesus[1], the very first question he asked the disciples he found there was:

> *Did you receive the Holy Spirit when you believed?*

The same sense of urgency is seen in Acts 8 where we read that as soon as the apostles heard that the Samaritans had become Christians they sent to them Peter and John so that they might receive the Holy Spirit (vv 14-16).

The apostles knew the difference the Holy Spirit had made in their own lives. Jesus himself had commanded them not to leave Jerusalem until they had received this gift that the Father had promised which would give them power enabling them to be his witnesses to the ends of the earth (Acts 1:4-8).

The apostles knew too that this gift was not just for them, but for their converts and their converts' converts, in fact *to as many as the Lord our God shall call* (Acts 2:38). The gift of the Spirit is the rightful inheritance of every true Christian and the New Testament indicates how very simply that gift may be received.

The Holy Spirit is a Gift

First, it is clear that the Holy Spirit is a gift. Jesus promised that our heavenly Father would *give* the Spirit to those who ask him (Luke 11:13) and Acts too frequently refers to the

---

[1] Acts 19:1-7

Spirit as a gift[1]. In this connection, it is important that we understand two things:

The gift cannot be earned

If the Holy Spirit is a gift then there is no way we can earn the right to receive him. Many Christians are held back from receiving the Spirit because of a sense of their own unworthiness. They feel the need to achieve a certain level of holiness before they will ask God for the gift of his Spirit. But Acts makes it clear that the Spirit was given to young converts. Their only holiness came from their repentance and faith in Christ.

It is of course true that we are not worthy to receive the Spirit. We never will be! But neither are we worthy to enter heaven. Our certainty of eternal life depends not on our own righteousness but on Christ's atoning work on the cross. In response to our repentance and faith in what Christ did for us at Calvary God has declared us righteous. He looks on us as though we had never sinned at all. That is what justification means. It is God who, by his grace, has made us fit for heaven, and because of his grace and forgiveness we may *receive* (not *earn* or *merit*) the gift of the Spirit[2]. In short, if our justification makes us fit for heaven, it certainly makes us fit to receive the Spirit.

The gift has already been given

And there is no longer any need for us to wait for the gift. It is true that before Pentecost the disciples were told to wait (Acts 1:4), but that was because the Spirit was not yet given (John 7:39). But at Pentecost the waiting period was over. The gift was given.

---

[1] Acts 2:38, 5:32, 8:20, 10:45, 11:17

[2] In Paul's writings the Spirit is seen as a foretaste of heaven. See for example Ephesians 1:13. More will be said about his in a later chapter.

The child who has been promised a present for its birthday must wait to receive it. But when its birthday has come, there is no more waiting. The gift is there to be taken! In some ways Pentecost was the birthday of the Church and ever since, thank God, the gift has been there to be taken. After Pentecost we never find a single occasion when Christians waited for the gift of the Spirit. The gift was, and is, available to all for at Pentecost the Spirit was poured out *on all people* (Acts 2:17)[1].

How to Receive the Gift

So how may we receive the gift? Acts 2:38 makes it clear that the promise is for all who will *Repent and be baptised*[2]. So what more must we do to receive the Spirit?

The answer to this question is found in John 7:37-39 where Jesus said that once the Spirit had been given anyone who was thirsty might come to him and drink. The key here is coming to Jesus. He is the one who baptises with the Holy Spirit[3]. As we come to him, thirsty for the Spirit, we should come for cleansing if we need it, we should come expecting, and we should come in worship.

But before we look at each of these aspects a little more closely it is important to note that in the Book of Acts the Spirit was sometimes received through the laying on of hands.

---

[1] This does not mean, of course, that all people have received the Spirit. It signifies that as from Pentecost the Spirit, who previously had been given to relatively few chosen individuals for a specific purpose, was now available to all.

[2] The gift of the Spirit was, as we have seen, usually received at/after baptism. However, baptism must not be seen as an absolute condition for receiving the Spirit, as the case of Cornelius (Acts 10:44-4 8) makes clear. It is noteworthy, however, that he *was* baptised immediately after receiving the Spirit.

[3] Matthew 3:11, Mark 1:8, Luke 3:16, John 1:33.

The Laying on of Hands

As we look at the four incidents in Acts where we are told about groups of people receiving the baptism in the Spirit[1] it is interesting to note that on two of these occasions the Spirit was received through the laying on of hands. It was *through the laying on of the apostles' hands* that the Samaritans received the Spirit (Acts 8:17-18), and the Spirit came on the Ephesians *when Paul placed his hands on them* (Acts 19:6). Indeed Paul himself was filled with the Spirit when Ananias laid his hands on him (Acts 9:17) although Luke's account here is less detailed than in the other passages.

In fact it was only at Pentecost and at Caesarea that the Spirit was received without the laying on of hands and it might be argued that there were special reasons for this on both occasions. Pentecost was the first occasion for Jesus' disciples to receive the Spirit and so there was no-one to lay hands on them. In the case of Cornelius those receiving the Spirit were Gentiles and the fact that the Spirit was given without the laying on of hands could well be understood as a further token that God had accepted them (Acts 10:47, 11:15-18).

From this it should be assumed that the normal means of receiving the Spirit is through the laying on of hands, although people are sometimes baptized in the Spirit without it if the Lord has some special purpose in their situation. Generally speaking, then, if you're seeking the baptism in the Spirit, I would encourage you to ask for the laying on of hands. As you do so, it will help if you come in the following way.

Come for cleansing

As we have already seen, we can never be good enough in our own righteousness to receive the gift of God's *Holy* Spirit. But because of our faith in Christ we have been justified

[1] Acts 2:4, 8:14ff, 10:44ff, 19:1-7.

(Romans 5:1). God has declared us righteous despite our unworthiness and it is only in that righteousness with which he has credited us that we are fit to receive the Spirit.

Yet despite this we may well still feel the need for forgiveness as we come to Jesus asking him for the gift of the Spirit. In this connection it is always helpful to remember 1 John 1:9. If we confess our sin to him he will forgive us and cleanse us from all unrighteousness.

Come expecting

Now that we are freshly cleansed from our sin we may expect God to fill us with his Spirit. Jesus' promise in Luke 11 is a source of great encouragement here. The passage teaches us two main truths. First, if we ask for the Holy Spirit God will give us the Holy Spirit, and second, when as children of God we ask for the Spirit God will not let us receive 'stones' or 'scorpions' or 'snakes'.

So when we ask for the Spirit we must expect to receive the Spirit. Our heavenly Father won't let us get the wrong thing! He does not allow his children to receive harmful, counterfeit, or satanic gifts. He does not deal in demons! When his children ask for the Spirit, it is the Spirit he gives.

Let us then ask for the Spirit and expect to receive. Let us also expect to speak in tongues, which is the evidence the Spirit initially gives us. In this connection please notice that speaking in tongues is something *you* do. The Holy Spirit does not speak in tongues - you do. Paul says

> *If I pray in an unknown tongue, my spirit prays........*[1].

---

[1] 1 Corinthians 14:14. Cf v 27 and the passages in Acts where *they* spoke in tongues (2:4, 10:46, 19:6)

Nowhere does the Bible refer to the Holy Spirit speaking in tongues. He enables us to do so (Acts 2:4). He makes sure that the right sounds come out of our mouths. But it is *we* who speak in tongues, and it is when in faith we begin to praise God in this way that we begin to *pray with the spirit* as distinct from *with the mind*[1].

Come to Jesus in worship

The disciples who were filled with the Spirit on the Day of Pentecost had spent time in prayer (Acts 1:14), but they had also spent time in worship (Luke 24:49-53). Jesus had told them that the Holy Spirit would come, and it seems that the disciples not only prayed for his coming but praised God that he would come. Jesus had said, *If I go, I will send him to you* (John 16:7). The source of the disciples' joy as they waited for the coming of the Holy Spirit was that Jesus *had* gone!

They had seen him go. He had told them that they would be baptised in the Holy Spirit *in a few days* (Acts 1:5). They would receive power for witnessing when the Spirit came (v8). And then, *he was taken up before their very eyes* (v9). They saw him go into heaven (v11).

They had never seen him like this before! They had seen him as a carpenter, a teacher, a miracle-worker, even as the Messiah. They had come to see him as *the Christ, the Son of the living God,* and eventually, after his resurrection, as *Lord and God.* But always God upon earth. Now their gaze was lifted heavenward, far above all rule and authority, power and dominion, and every title that can be given, not only in the present age but also in the age to come!

Christ is ascended. He is King. He is Lord. He is God. He reigns in heaven, he reigns over the earth. All things are by

---

[1] 1 Corinthians 14:14ff

him and through him and for him and to him. He is before all things and by him all things exist. Jesus of Nazareth is Lord of the universe! No wonder they worshipped!

Will *you* worship him? Worship him with your mind, but worship with your spirit too. Begin by faith to utter those new-found words of praise upon your lips. As you begin to speak, the Spirit will enable you. Yes, come to Jesus. Come for cleansing. Come expecting. Come in worship and adoration. Jesus is glorified. The Spirit has been given. If you are thirsty, come and drink!

Maintaining the Fulness of the Spirit

Once we have received the gift of the Spirit, the Bible makes it clear that the responsibility for maintaining it is ours. The Ephesians who, after they had believed, were sealed with the Holy Spirit (Ephesians 1:13), were commanded to maintain the experience by being constantly filled with the Spirit (5:18). Similarly Paul tells Timothy

> *Fan into flame the gift of God which is in you through the laying on of my hands. For God did not give us a spirit of timidity, but a spirit of power, of love and of self-discipline* (2 Timothy 1:6-7).

From these verses it is clear that although Timothy had originally received the Spirit through the laying on of Paul's hands, Paul did not expect him to need continual ministry in this connection. Once he had received the Spirit's fire, Timothy was responsible for keeping it burning himself.

Feelings and Phenomena

We are living at a time when great emphasis is being placed on physical phenomena as evidences of the Spirit's presence. But though many have undoubtedly testified to great blessing as a result of such experiences[1], the Bible actually says very little about *feeling* the Spirit's power and it certainly does not encourage us to go back meeting after meeting to 'get some more' by going forward again and again for prayer.

Of course we may be stirred emotionally, as when the disciples were filled with joy as well as with the Spirit (Acts 13:52). We may even experience powerful physical sensations when the Spirit comes upon us - it is possible that the disciples appeared to be drunk on the Day of Pentecost, though the context does not demand such an interpretation[2]. However, any physical sensations we *may* experience when we are first filled with the Spirit will not necessarily accompany subsequent infillings. When seeking to receive or to maintain the fulness of the Spirit we should not look or wait for physical or emotional phenomena. These may come, but the Spirit is essentially received by *faith* and not by feelings.

So how *do* we maintain the fulness of the Spirit day by day? We do so by using the gift God has given us for the purposes for which it was given - prayer, worship, and witness.

Prayer

The disciples were first filled with the Spirit while praying (Acts 1:14, 2:1-4) and it was while they were praying that

---

[1] I refer to such extra-biblical phenomena such as falling down, laughter etc. which at the time of writing are captivating the attention of the secular as well as the Christian press.

[2] Much has been made of this, but the passage at no point states that the disciples appeared to be drunk. That was what those who made fun of them accused them of. It may well have been the only possible explanation they could come up with for the miracle of tongues, for that is the context in which the statement was made. It would be extremely unwise to read into this passage the kind of 'drunken' phenomena we are hearing of today. Perhaps we need to remember that self-control is part of the fruit which the Spirit produces. See Galatians 5:23. Cf 2 Timothy 1:7.

they were filled again (Acts 4:31). Our prayer-life is of great importance in this matter of maintaining the fulness of the Spirit. We should, of course, pray with the mind in our own mother-tongue, but we should also pray with the spirit in other tongues. Having spoken in tongues when initially filled with the Spirit we should daily fan the gift into flame, building ourselves up spiritually. In 1 Corinthians 14:4 Paul tells us that he who speaks in a tongue edifies himself and Jude 20 encourages us to build ourselves up in our most holy faith and pray in the Holy Spirit.

We need to remember that speaking in tongues is not something that happens to us. It is something we do. Just as we deliberately pray with our mind we should deliberately pray with our spirit (in tongues). And we should do so regularly and frequently.

Worship

Worship too is important as we seek to maintain the fulness of the Spirit. Paul says

> *Be filled with the Spirit. Speak to one another with psalms, hymns, and spiritual songs. Sing and make music in your heart to the Lord* (Ephesians 5:18-19).

Both public and private worship are suggested here in connection with maintaining the fulness of the Spirit[1] and it is sad that some Christians seem to give expression to worship

---

[1] The Greek may be translated *Speaking to yourselves* rather than *Speak to one another*. Either translation is valid, but the former could suggest that a private context is in mind. *Singing and making music in one's heart* certainly suggests this. The *spiritual songs* may well refer to singing in tongues which in 1 Corinthians 14:15 is defined as singing with one's spirit. If so, the context may well be private rather than public, bearing in mind Paul's general cautions about the public use of tongues in 1 Corinthians 14.

only when in public. The Spirit-filled life is filled with praise, in private as well as in public and again the gift of tongues will help us, for we may *sing with the spirit* in addition to praying with the spirit[1]. One function of speaking in tongues is to magnify God (Acts 10:46) and as such it is a valuable aid to worship, especially when the greatness of God seems too much for our natural language to express.

Yet tongues is not only valuable for the mountain-top experiences of the Christian life. It is also extremely precious in the valleys. When we are feeling spiritually low we usually do not feel like speaking in tongues. Indeed, there is the temptation to believe that it would be irreverent or even blasphemous to speak in tongues when we are in such a low spiritual condition. But that is just the time we need to. Speaking in tongues builds us up (1 Corinthians 14:4). Paul does not say that we will *feel* edified, but he does say that we will *be* edified! Our daily prayer time should therefore include a praise time. We do not always feel like praising God, but we should *bless the Lord at all times*. Whatever our circumstances, God is always worthy of our worship.

Witness

Another purpose for which God has filled us with the Spirit is that we might be witnesses (Acts 1:8). The Holy Spirit will never force us to witness for Christ, but he will empower our witness when we do so. It is not surprising that some Christians fail to maintain the fulness of the Spirit when they fail to use the gift for the purpose for which it has been given. Every true Christian should want to tell others about Jesus, and the Holy Spirit gives us the power to do so. If we will obey his commands, he will confirm our word, and those who need Jesus will be enabled to find him.

---

[1] 1 Corinthians 14:14-15

CHAPTER EIGHT

The Gifts of the Spirit

Once we have received the baptism in the Holy Spirit we must guard against the danger of feeling that we have 'arrived'. The baptism in the Spirit is not an end in itself. In fact it's just a beginning. It's a gateway through which we enter into an entirely new realm - the supernatural. It is God's will for us that having initially spoken in tongues, we might also go on to exercise other supernatural gifts of the Spirit[1].

These are mentioned in 1 Corinthians 12 where Paul lists nine gifts (vv 8-10) and tells us that he does not want us to be ignorant about them (v 1). It would not be possible within the scope of this chapter to deal with each of these gifts in detail, but we will seek to outline what the New Testament teaches about them in general, considering their nature, origin, and purpose, before suggesting how they may be received and used.

Their Nature

They are Gifts

In 1 Corinthians 12:4 we are told that there are different kinds of *gifts* but the same Spirit. The Greek word used here is *charismata*[2]. This comes from the word *charis* which means

---

[1] Correctly understood, 1 Corinthians 12:13 teaches us that we have been baptised in the Spirit for the benefit of the body. As this is set in the context of spiritual gifts, the clear implication is that one purpose of the baptism in the Holy Spirit is that we might be a blessing to our fellow-Christians as we press forward to exercise these gifts. Cf pp 68-70.

[2] This is the plural form. The singular is *charisma.*

'grace'. The emphasis is that these are gifts that God has given us because of his grace. Although the gifts referred to here are described as *spiritual* (v1), the word *charisma* is also used to refer to *natural* gifts. In 1 Corinthians 7:7, for example, Paul calls celibacy a *charisma* and in Romans 12:6-8 the *charismata* he lists seem to be a mixture of *spiritual* gifts like prophecy and *natural* gifts such as contributing to the needs of others[1].

Another interesting use of the word *charisma* is to be found in Romans 6:23 where the word refers to *the gift of God* which *is eternal life in Christ Jesus our Lord.* We know that we certainly cannot earn this gift by our own human merit but must gratefully receive it by faith. It is a *charisma.* It springs from God's grace. And just as we cannot earn our salvation we must recognise too that we cannot earn spiritual gifts. They are not given us because of our own righteousness or holiness. They are given because of God's grace.

The Corinthians are a clear example of this principle. They were not lacking in spiritual gifts (1 Corinthians 1:7), but this was certainly not because they were particularly holy. Paul calls them *worldly* (3:3) because of their jealousy and quarrelling, rebukes them for tolerating immorality (5:1-12), and accuses them of drunkenness at the Lord's Supper (11:21). Their example, although of course not one to be followed, illustrates very clearly that spiritual gifts are not given because of human merit but because of God's wonderful grace.

---

[1] From this it is clear that not all *charismata* are supernatural. However it appears that those listed in 1 Corinthans 12:8-10 are. The context suggests this and the fact that Paul also refers to these particular gifts as *pneumatika* (v 1) may also indicate this. Cf pp 91ff.

Now from this we can learn two very important lessons. First, we must not assume that because a person is used in the exercise of spiritual gifts they are more holy than other Christians. Sadly the opposite is sometimes the case. And second, we should not hold back from seeking spiritual gifts for ourselves because we are conscious of our own shortcomings. Of course we should seek to live holy lives, but we will never be holy enough to merit God's gifts. If he has been gracious enough to save us from our sin, if he has been gracious enough to baptise us with his Spirit, then he will surely not withhold any good gift which will bless us or make us a blessing. *All* his gifts spring from his grace.

They are Spiritual

But the gifts listed in 1 Corinthians 12 are not only gifts. They are *spiritual* gifts (v1). Here Paul describes them as *pneumatika*. This word has a variety of shades of meaning but in the context clearly indicates that the gifts Paul speaks of come from the Holy Spirit himself[1] . This is what distinguishes them from the natural *charismata* mentioned elsewhere. These particular *charismata* are not natural. They are also *pneumatika.* They are spiritual.

There is also a strong suggestion that they are supernatural. Speaking in tongues, for example, cannot possibly refer to natural linguistic ability. It is, rather, as Acts 2 makes perfectly clear, the ability to speak a language one has never learned through the supernatural inspiration of the Holy Spirit. This point is also backed up by Hebrews 2:4 where we read that God himself testified to the validity of the Gospel message *by signs, wonders and various miracles, and gifts of the Holy Spirit distributed according to his will.* The mention of the gifts of the Spirit along with supernatural phenomena like

---

[1] The gifts are called *pneumatika* because they come from the *Pneuma* (Spirit) himself. See also vv 7-11 which demonstrate that the gifts come from the Holy Spirit.

signs and wonders and miracles clearly indicates that the gifts themselves are supernatural.

From this we may learn two more important lessons. If the gifts are supernatural there is no limit to what God may accomplish through them. Through the gifts of the Spirit the church of Jesus Christ has available to it the miracle-working power of the true and living God! And, equally wonderfully, because the gifts are supernatural there is no limit as to the persons God may give them to. They may be exercised by weak and strong, rich and poor, able and less able, young and old alike! They are not received in accordance with our natural ability. They are supernatural endowments from the Spirit.

They are Manifestations

Finally, in 1 Corinthians 12:7 the gifts are referred to as *manifestations.* The Greek word *phanerosis* which is used here literally means 'a clear display, an outward evidencing of a latent principle'. Just as the light which shines from the light-bulb is an outward evidence of the electricity at work within it, so spiritual gifts are an outward display of the Holy Spirit at work within us. We may speak a language we have never learned because the omniscient Spirit lives within us. Miracles are possible because the Almighty fills our being.

Once again we can learn two lessons from this. Spiritual gifts do not come from God in outer space! They come from the God who lives within us. They are well within our reach! But if we are expecting to manifest them we must keep filled with the Spirit. If the light is to shine, the electricity is to be kept flowing. But that leads us to the question of the origin of the gifts - where they come from.

Their origin

Amazing miracles took place in the early church. Each new convert was expected to receive the baptism in the Holy Spirit and to speak in tongues, so every individual Christian, right from the start, had a personal experience of the supernatural. In fact the miraculous was so common that in Acts 19 Luke talks about *special miracles* which God did through Paul - *special* miracles - not the ordinary kind that they were used to!

So the first Christians were no strangers to the supernatural. When Paul wrote to the Corinthians he mentioned nine 'spiritual gifts'[1] and knew that the Corinthians would know what he was talking about. His reason for writing was that they were using the gifts badly and he needed to bring correction into the situation. That's probably why he didn't stop to give a definition for each gift. The Corinthians knew what they were. They just didn't know how to exercise them properly. To do so they needed to understand the purpose for which the gifts are given. They also needed to be aware that not every supernatural manifestation comes from the Holy Spirit.

We must never assume that all miraculous phenomena are attributable to the power of the Holy Spirit. Satan has his miracle-workers too! As we read the opening verses of 1 Corinthians 12 it is clear that Paul is very anxious that his readers should be able to distinguish the genuine from the counterfeit, the divine from the demonic. He did not want them to be ignorant about these things (v 1) and reminded them that before they had become Christians they had been idol-worshippers (v 2). This meant that they had been involved with the demonic[2] and although they themselves had

---

[1] 1 Corinthians 12:8-10. Paul does refer to other gifts elsewhere, but the gifts listed here are distinctly supernatural.

[2] 1 Corinthians 10:19-21.

been delivered from Satan's power there was always the possibility that unbelievers might come into their meetings[1] and, in the free atmosphere that prevailed in the Corinthian church, might actually seek to exercise some spiritual gift.

It was vital, therefore, that the Corinthians should be able to distinguish the true from the false - as indeed it is still vital today - and so Paul warned them that

> *No-one who is speaking by the Spirit of God says 'Jesus be cursed' and no-one can say 'Jesus is Lord' except by the Holy Spirit* (v 3).

Here we are given a clear means of testing the origin of a supernatural manifestation. Does the user of the gift in question acknowledge the lordship of Jesus? If not, he is not of God. It is God's revealed will that

> *at the name of Jesus every knee should bow in heaven and on earth and under the earth and every tongue confess that Jesus Christ is Lord to the glory of God the Father*[2].

Those who refuse to acknowledge that lordship are not of God, however pleasant their personality, however plausible their arguments, and however powerful their miracles. Spiritual realities are eternally valid and the test Paul gave the Corinthians nearly 2,000 years ago is applicable today. A 'Christian' spiritualist may pay lip service to Christ in the course of conversation, but will not, in fact can not, say *Jesus is Lord* while controlled by a spirit-guide in the course of a seance.

---

[1] That this was to be expected is clear from 1 Corinthians 14:23-25.
[2] Philippians 2:10-11.

A further interesting difference between the 'gifts' of spiritism and the gifts of the Holy Spirit is made clear in 1 Corinthians 12:4-11. Spiritist mediums with a variety of 'gifts' will acknowledge that they receive them from a variety of spirits. One familiar spirit will give the gifts of healing, another gift of tongues, and yet another the gift of prophecy, and so on. The medium who exercises three gifts receives them from three spirits! That is something quite different from the gifts listed in 1 Corinthians 12. All nine of these gifts are given by the *one, same* Holy Spirit[1] .

Finally, before leaving the subject of the counterfeit, let it be clearly understood that no true Christian need fear that his gifts are demonic. Our heavenly Father not only *gives the Holy Spirit to those who ask him* (Luke 11:13). He also gives *good gifts* (Matthew 7:11). Demons tremble in the presence of Christ. They have nothing at all to do with him (Mark 1:24). If Christ dwells in our hearts by faith we have nothing to fear, for

> *the one who is in you is greater than the one who is in the world* (1 John 4:4).

A true Christian is one who can say from the heart that *Jesus is Lord* (Romans 10:9), and no-one can say *Jesus is Lord* except by the Holy Spirit (1 Corinthians 12:3). Since this is the test that Paul gives us for distinguishing between true and false gifts, it follows that no true Christian can exercise a demonically inspired gift.

[1] Notice how the phrase *the same Spirit* recurs repeatedly in verses 4-11.

Their Purpose

But of course it's possible for a Christian to use a genuine gift for the wrong purpose. This was precisely what was wrong with the Corinthians. They were using their gifts for their own personal edification instead of for the edification of others[1]. That's why Paul stresses the importance of using gifts for the good of others. Their major purpose is for the edification of the church. The manifestation of the Spirit is given *for the common good* (1 Corinthians 12:7). We've been baptised in the Spirit *for the benefit of the body* (1 Corinthians 12:13)[2] and the value of a gift is determined by the measure in which it edifies the church, for

> *He who prophesies is greater than he who speaks in tongues, unless he interprets, so that the church may be edified* (1 Corinthians 14:5).

And Paul longed to see the Romans so that he might impart some spiritual gift *to make them strong* (Romans 1:11).

We'll be saying more about this in a moment, but before concluding this section, it is important to note that spiritual gifts are also of great importance in evangelism[3]. When Jesus commanded his disciples to go into all the world and preach the gospel to all creation, he promised them that miraculous signs would accompany the preaching of the word (Mark 16:17-18). Mark 16:20 tells us that this in fact took place and

---

[1] Cf 1 Corinthians 14 where Paul seeks to correct this tendency.

[2] The common translation 'into one body' is misleading and unhelpful. Paul is not discussing entrance into the body here, but how we function *within* it. The Greek preposition *eis* may properly be translated *for* rather than *into* (as is customary here). Cf 1 Corinthians 8:6 and Ephesians 4:30 where NIV translates *eis* as *for*. Cf pp 68-70.

[3] In Corinthians Paul confines his discussion to their purpose in the church for that was the immediate problem at Corinth. Elsewhere it is clear, however, that he recognised their great value in evangelism.

the Book of Acts continues the story with a catalogue of miracles that confirmed the message of the early disciples. God himself testified to it

> *by signs, wonders and various miracles and gifts of the Holy Spirit distributed according to his will* (Hebrews 2:4).

Paul could speak of what Christ had accomplished through him in leading the Gentiles to obey God, by what he had said and done

> *by the power of signs and miracles through the power of the Spirit*[1],

adding

> *So from Jerusalem all the way round to Illyricum I have fully proclaimed the gospel of Christ,*

thereby suggesting that the gospel is not 'fully proclaimed' unless it is attested by signs from heaven[2].

How we need to pray and believe, like the disciples in Acts 4:29-31, that God will stretch out his hand to heal and that signs and wonders may be done in the name of Jesus so that God's servants might speak his word with boldness! Spiritual gifts make evangelism effective.

---

[1] Romans 15:18-19

[2] For a defense of this interpretation (despite the commentaries) consult my PhD Thesis, *Healing and the Atonement,* Nottingham, 1993, p 220.

Receiving Spiritual Gifts

Spiritual gifts are of great importance, therefore, both for evangelism and for the edification of the church. It is, therefore, essential that we understand how they may be received. In this connection it is vital to remember that our *only* source for faith and practice must always be the word of God. A tremendous amount of misunderstanding can arise as a result of people listening to accounts of how others have received the baptism or gifts of the Spirit if their experience in these matters is not compared with and verified by what God has revealed in the Scriptures.

As a simple example, someone with the gift of prophecy may tell us that when the Holy Spirit inspires him to prophesy, he sees the words he is to speak written out, as if on a blackboard, before his eyes. Now it would be quite wrong to suggest that a prophecy cannot be received in this way, but it would be equally wrong to imply that the gift is always imparted in such a manner. For some, it would seem, the gift comes not visually but audibly, while for others - probably the great majority - a strong impression is felt in the spirit that certain things need to be said to God's people. God seems to deal with different people in different ways, but he never acts in a way that contradicts the Bible.

In discussing how we may receive the gifts of the Spirit, then, we must be careful to say no more than what the Bible says. Once we have said that we must leave the matter to the Holy Spirit who distributes the gifts just as he determines (1 Corinthians 12:11). This immediately raises the thorny question as to whether one Christian can be instrumental in imparting a spiritual gift to another.

Can Spiritual Gifts be Imparted?

The main basis for the view that spiritual gifts can be imparted[1] is Romans 1:11 where Paul says:

> *I long to see you so that I may impart to you some spiritual gift to make you strong.*

The phrase used for *spiritual gift* here is *charisma pneumatikon* and this certainly lends support to the view that Paul is referring to the same kind of gifts as he lists in 1 Corinthians 12:8-10, for these gifts are described both as *charismata* (v 4) and as *pneumatika* (v 1). Indeed, they are the only gifts described as both *charismata* and *pneumatika* in the New Testament and so the inference is very strong that it was one of these gifts that Paul wanted to impart to the Romans. The main objection seems to be, however, that since Paul says that spiritual gifts are given as the Holy Spirit determines (v 11) how can a man be instrumental in their impartation?

The answer to this question must surely be that, provided that a person is truly led by the Spirit in praying for another to receive a particular spiritual gift, there is a sense in which they may be said to have imparted that gift. By way of illustration of this general principle we might consider the case of miraculous healings. When the sick are healed it is of course God, not man, who heals (Acts 3:12). Yet in Matthew 10:8 Jesus told his disciples to *heal the sick.* So was it God or the disciples who were doing the healing? The answer of course is both! In the ultimate sense it is God who alone who can heal, but because of the power God has graciously given his servants, they do 'heal' at his command.

---

[1] 1Timothy 4:14 is also sometimes quoted in this connection.

A similar parallel may be drawn with the baptism in the Holy Spirit. It is Jesus who is the baptizer[1] and yet we read in Acts 8:18 that the Spirit was given through the laying on of the apostles' hands. There was, therefore, a sense in which Peter and John imparted the Spirit to the Samaritans. But this does not contradict the overall truth that it is God who gives us his Spirit.

In the light of this I take the view that it is perfectly proper, if you are seeking, for example, the gift of prophecy, to ask someone who already exercises that gift to pray for you that you might exercise it too. In doing so, however, you should remember that it is the Spirit himself who distributes the gifts as he determines, and therefore to give God alone the glory if you receive it. But apart from asking for prayer in this matter, what else may we do to receive spiritual gifts?

A Right Attitude

In seeking for spiritual gifts it is obviously important that we have a right attitude towards them. We need to understand what we're asking for. We need to remember that they are *gifts* that come as a result of God's grace. We cannot earn the right to possess them. We should remember, too, that they are *spiritual* gifts that come from the Holy Spirit. We therefore need to keep full of the Spirit. As we are full of him the Spirit will *manifest* himself through us in ways that please him.

We should also bear in mind the purpose for which the gifts are given. We should examine our motives asking ourselves exactly why we wish to receive them. If we will remember that the gifts are spiritual manifestations[2] of the Holy Spirit within us, given for the purpose of confirming the gospel

---

[1] See Matthew 3:11, Mark 1:8, Luke 3:16, John 1:33.

[2] See 1 Corinthians 12:7. See also p 90.

message or for the edification of our fellow-believers, we may expect him to give us what he knows is best. Yet although the gifts are distributed as the Holy Spirit determines, that does not take away our responsibility in the matter. The gifts are not some optional extra for which we may pray if we happen to be interested! We are told to desire them eagerly![1]

Right Actions

And of course if we really desire something eagerly we will do all that we can to get it! So what can we *do* to receive spiritual gifts? First, Paul tells us that we should *pray*. Those who speak in tongues are instructed to pray for the gift of interpretation[2] and although it is only one specific gift that is referred to here it would seem that if prayer is encouraged as a means of obtaining one gift it must also be appropriate to pray for the others.

Second, we must exercise *faith*. Tongues and healings for example are promised to *those who believe* (Mark 16:17,18) and those who prophesy must do so *in proportion to their faith* (Romans 12:6). We must not only *ask* for the gifts in prayer, but also *believe* that God will give them, remembering that faith without works is dead, and that if we really believe we will *act*. God is more willing to give than we are to receive. If we really want him to use us in evangelism or in edifying the church, we should desire the gifts, ask for the gifts, believe for the gifts, and move forward in faith to use them.

The Right Atmosphere

Finally, perhaps it is worth mentioning that, since the gifts are given for the edification of the church, and as it seems unlikely

---

[1] 1 Corinthians 12:31, 14:1, 12.

[2] 1 Corinthians 14:13.

that any gift would be manifested in a church that denies their validity or underestimates their importance, if we are really serious in our desire to make progress in the realm of spiritual gifts, we will see to it that we worship where the Spirit is not quenched.

That is to say, if we are to receive spiritual gifts and develop in our use of them so that others can be helped and built up, we need to fellowship in a church where the leadership not only believes in but also understands and encourages the use of the gifts. In the right kind of spiritual atmosphere spiritual gifts flow naturally and easily. It is not difficult to have the faith to prophesy in a fellowship where believers love each other and want to edify one another and where the leadership will sympathetically encourage us and, if necessary, lovingly correct us as we seek to move forward in faith.

CHAPTER NINE

The Spirit in the Church

Most of what we have said so far has been to do with our personal experience of the Spirit as individuals. In this chapter we will turn our attention to the work of the Spirit in the church. Pentecost was undoubtedly a personal experience, for each of those present was filled with the Holy Spirit. Tongues of fire came to rest on *each of them*. But it was also a corporate experience. The sound like the blowing of a violent wind *filled the whole house* where they were sitting. They were *all* filled with the Holy Spirit.

This suggests that not only do we need to enjoy our own personal experience of the Spirit in our daily lives but that we also need to see the power of the Spirit manifested as we gather together regularly in our local church.

Temples of the Spirit

In this connection it is interesting that the apostle Paul sees both the individual Christian and the local church as a 'temple' of the Holy Spirit, thus underlining the importance of the Spirit's work at both individual and corporate level.

Our Bodies as Temples

In 1 Corinthians 6:19-20 we read that our bodies are temples of the Holy Spirit who lives in us and whom we have received as a gift from God. We are reminded that we are not our own because Jesus paid a great price for us when he died to save us from our sin. So we are encouraged to honour God with our bodies.

The teaching in this passage is very clear. Paul has been warning the Corinthians that they must not commit sexual immorality and one of the reasons he gives is that our bodies are temples of the Holy Spirit. As such they are holy and we must be careful not to defile them with unclean behaviour[1].

The Church as a Temple

But Paul also describes the church as a temple of the Spirit. In Ephesians 2 we read how the Gentiles who

> *were once excluded from citizenship in Israel and foreigners to the covenants of the promise... have been brought near through the blood of Christ* (vv12-13).

Christ himself is our peace and has made both Jew and Gentile one because he has

> *destroyed the barrier, the dividing wall of hostility* (v 14).

This is a clear reference to the stone wall in the Jewish temple which divided the Court of the Gentiles from the temple proper. It carried an inscription in both Latin and Greek which 'forbade any foreigner to go in under pain of death'[2]. But now, through Christ, both Jew and Gentile have access to the Father by the Holy Spirit (v 18).

Indeed, because of Christ's death on the cross and through the work of the Spirit, both Jew and Gentile are part of a new

---

[1] As we shall see later, he says something similar with regard to the church as the temple of the Spirit in 1 Corinthians 3:16-17.

[2] See Josephus, *Antiquities,* xv 11. 5 and *The Wars of the Jews* v 5. 2, vi. 2. 4. Foulkes notes that such an inscription was discovered by the French archaeologist, M. Clermont Ganneau, in 1871 (Foulkes, F., *Ephesians,* London, IVP, 1963, p.81). Cf Acts 21:29ff.

temple God is building. The apostles and prophets are its foundation and Jesus himself is the chief cornerstone and the whole building, with both Jews and Gentiles as components, is being joined together and rising to become *a holy temple in the Lord ... a dwelling in which God lives by his Spirit* (vv 19-22).

From this we can learn three things. First, it is clear that God's temple is no longer a building. God's dwelling place is not a temple or cathedral made of stone. By his Spirit he inhabits the company of the redeemed. The 'church' is not the *place* we go to on Sundays, but the company of *people* who gather there in Jesus' name.

Second, we learn that membership of the church (being part of God's true temple) is not dependent on ethnic or religious background, but simply on being 'in Christ'. It is 'in Christ' that the Gentiles have been brought near (v 13). It is 'in him' (v 21) that the different parts of God's temple are joined together. And it is *in Christ Jesus* that we have been created to do the works which God has prepared for us to do (v 10). Whether we be Jew or Gentile it is only if we are 'in Christ' that we are part of his church[1].

Finally, we discover that being part of the church is a very serious and yet a very wonderful thing. This 'temple' God is building is 'holy' (v 21), a place where God lives by his Spirit (v 22). This truth is reinforced by the choice of the Greek word Paul uses for 'temple' here. In Greek there are two main words for 'temple'. One is *hieron,* the other is *naos. Hieron* was usually used to signify the temple as a whole, including all its outer courts and precincts, whereas *naos* would generally

---

[1] The theme of being *in Christ* is very strong in Paul's writings, especially in Ephesians. Cf Ephesians 1:1, 3, 4, 7, 9, 11, 13, 20, 2:6, 10, 13, 21, 22 etc. It is probably Paul's most common way of referring to a Christian.

refer to the innermost shrine. In a pagan temple this would be thought to be the dwelling place of the god to whom the temple was dedicated. In the Jewish temple it would be the Holy of Holies.

The fact that Paul uses *naos* rather than *hieron* here to refer to the church as God's temple may very well suggest that he sees the church as God's Holy of Holies. Not only may Christians have confidence to *enter* the Most Holy Place by the blood of Jesus (Hebrews 10:19), but the church actually *becomes* the dwelling-place of God through the Spirit!

This most solemn and awesome thought is underlined by what Paul teaches the Corinthians:

> *Don't you know that you yourselves are God's temple (naos) and that God's Spirit lives in you? If anyone destroys God's temple, God will destroy him; for God's temple is sacred, and **you are** that temple*
> (1 Corinthians 3:16-17)[1].

From this we learn that the local church - even a very imperfect local church like that of the Corinthians[2] - is to be thought of as a holy temple in which the Spirit of God abides. But this is no reason to be complacent. The fact that God dwells in his church is here used as a solemn warning to those who were destroying the church by their divisions. When we gather in Jesus' name the Spirit of God is present among us. This should cause us on the one hand to be careful that our

---

[1] Here Paul uses *naos* again to refer to the church. 'You are' is plural while 'temple' is singular. This means that Paul is not referring here to the individual Corinthians as temples of God's Spirit - although he does that in 1 Corinthians 6:19, as we have already seen - but to the Corinthian church as a whole. They, the church, were the temple.

[2] Paul accuses the Corinthians of division, immaturity, immorality, disorder, lack of love, and unsound doctrine, and yet he still calls them God's temple!

attitude and behaviour are pleasing to God, and on the other, to expect that the Spirit's power will be manifest among us. We are in the presence of God himself!

The Spirit in Church Worship

The facts to which we have just referred obviously have serious implications with regard to our understanding of church worship. If the church really is *a dwelling in which God lives by his Spirit* then we should expect the Holy Spirit to be leading, guiding and inspiring us every time we gather to worship the Lord Jesus Christ. There seems to have been little formal liturgy at the time of the writing of the New Testament[1] but rather a real sense of dependence on the Holy Spirit. Indeed the formality with which so many churches worship today is probably far removed from the Spirit-directed gatherings of the early Christians.

That is not to say, of course, that the early Christians always got it right. Indeed, had they done so, there would have been little need for Paul to write chapters 11 to 14 of 1 Corinthians in which he corrects the disorders in their public worship. From these chapters we learn that the Corinthians were not only dressed in a manner inappropriate to the culture of the day but, at the Lord's Supper, were behaving with total disregard for one another to the extent that some went hungry while others actually got drunk. Although they were a charismatic congregation possessing and exercising a variety of spiritual gifts, they had little idea as to how these should be regulated and clearly placed an exaggerated importance on the value of speaking in tongues while gathered as a church. It is difficult to imagine how any church could be so disordered today!

---

[1] One evidence of this is Paul's reversing the order in which he refers to the bread and wine. Cf 1 Corinthians10:16, 11:23-26.

Yet, although these chapters are addressed to an immature church which lacked understanding in several very basic matters, there is much that we can learn from Paul's teaching here, even if our situation does not appear to be comparable with that of the Corinthians, for the *principles* underlying Paul's teaching are valid for the church of every generation and in every culture.

Below I have listed what I consider some of those principles to be. I have done so without comment, as the application of the principle will vary from one situation to another. Those in church leadership, however, might do well to consider these principles and use them as a check-list by which to evaluate the church services for which they are responsible. In so doing they will, I believe, be making room for the Spirit to dwell within his temple, the church.

1. The church is a body and as such is made up of many different but inter-dependent parts (12:14-26).

2. Each part of the body is important, simply because God has put it there (12:18).

3. It is, therefore, important that each part of the body be allowed to function as God intends it to. *Everyone* has something to contribute (14:26).

4. Whatever contribution is made, it should be made in love, so that the other members of the body may be built up and encouraged (14:1, 3, 26).

5. There is a supernatural dimension to the worship of the church provided by the power of the Spirit. We have been baptised in the Spirit for the benefit of the body so that the other members of the body

may profit through the gifts[1] the Spirit gives us (12:1-13).

6. Not all supernatural manifestations come from the Spirit, however, and these must be tested and evaluated (12:1-3, 14:29)

7. All spiritual gifts are subject to the control of those manifesting them (14:32) and there are biblical instructions for the correct exercise of these gifts (14:26-40).

8. Everything should be done in a fitting and orderly way. God is not a God of disorder (14:33, 40, 11:1-22, 27-34).

9. The conversion of unbelievers is a priority. Church worship should be regulated, when unbelievers are present, so as to be conducive to their conversion (14: 23-25).

10. Christ's sacrificial death is central to the worship of the church (11:23-26).

Clearly much more could be said about the Spirit in the worship of the Church. But the ten principles outlined above, if prayerfully followed, will bring the church today back to the biblical norms of early charismatic Christianity and preserve it from the excesses to which such gatherings are prone[2]. In short, they will do much to bring any local church towards

---

[1] See the section on Spiritual Gifts. Cf pp 68ff on 1 Corinthians 12:13.

[2] In recent years, phenomena such as Christians barking like dogs, roaring like lions and uncontrollable laughter have been reported as 'manifestations' of the Spirit. It is important that the biblical principles we have been considering here are applied when evaluating such phenomena.

what God intends it to be, *a dwelling in which God lives by his Spirit.*

Before closing this section, however, perhaps one final point needs to be made. We sometimes hear it said that it is good that there is a variety of styles of worship in the Church today as the different styles suit people of different temperaments. While there is, no doubt, a measure of truth in this, it must be surely borne in mind that, if God is worthy of our worship at all, he is worthy of the worship which he himself desires. It may be that, in following the principles outlined above, we will come closer to offering God that kind worship, worship which is indeed *in spirit and in truth.*

The Spirit in Church Government

Finally we must briefly consider the Spirit's role in relation to church government. Detailed discussion of this complex subject will not be possible here but it is noteworthy that the early Christians acknowledged the authority of the Holy Spirit in this vitally important area of church life.

The apostles themselves, who were of course the very first leaders of the infant church, were men who were filled with the Spirit (Acts 2:4) and they clearly recognised that those who would serve the church in any leadership capacity would need the same Spirit-given ability.

An early example of this is the choice of the seven men (Acts 6:1-7) who were to administer the distribution of food to the widows. This account is widely held, probably correctly, to refer to the appointment of the first deacons, for, although the word *diakonos* (deacon) is not found in the text, *diakonia* (v 1) and *diakoneo* (v2) are. What is important here, however, is not the title given to these people (if any), but the qualification required of them if they were to fulfill a relatively simple function. They were all to be people who were witnessed to be *full of the Spirit and wisdom* (Acts 6:3).

A little later in Acts we find several references to *elders*[1]. Their role has been much debated, but it is evident that, in the early church at least, they were entrusted with pastoral responsibility for the flock. Indeed it seems likely that the elders in Acts were the people Paul referred to as *pastors* in Ephesians 4:11. Acts 20 indicates that the elders (v 17) were to 'be shepherds of the church' (v 28) which meant watching over the flock (v 27) of which *the Holy Spirit had made them* overseers[2]. From this it is clear that only the Holy Spirit can equip a person for a role in church leadership. The title is not important. What matters is whether or not leaders have been truly appointed by the Spirit and are people who understand the leading of the Spirit.

In this connection it is worth noting that the Council of Jerusalem (Acts 15) offers an excellent example of how the Holy Spirit can help church leaders in the sometimes difficult task of church government if they are sensitive to his voice. The apostles and elders had gathered together to discuss the controversial issue of the circumcision of Gentile Christians. The details of the discussion need not concern us here. What is significant is that, after lengthy debate, they were able to say

> *It seemed good to the Holy Spirit and to us* (v 28).

Finally, it is perhaps important to understand that the Book of Acts offers us no fixed model with regard to the government of the church. There is no single pattern to which the church

---

[1] See, for example, Acts 11:30, 14:23, 15:2, 4, 6, 22, 23, 16:4, 20:17.

[2] It is possible that 1 Corinthians 12:28 also contains a reference to elders. NIV refers to 'those with gifts of administration', but the Greek *kuberneseis* literally means 'helmsmen', perhaps indicating those who steered or directed the work of the church.

today must feel it should adhere. The government of the early church was dynamic rather than static, being sufficiently flexible to adapt to changing circumstances as it was led by the Holy Spirit. Local churches today must be willing for a similar flexibility.

CHAPTER TEN

The Holy Spirit and the Future

So far we have been considering the work of the Spirit in the past and in the present. We must now turn our attention to the future, for a number of New Testament passages suggest that there is a connection between what the Holy Spirit does for us now and what he will do in the age to come. Hebrews 6:4-5, for example, indicates that our present experience of the Holy Spirit is nothing less than a taste of the powers (miracles)[1] of the age to come, and Romans 8:11 backs this up by telling us:

> *... if the Spirit of him who raised Jesus from the dead is living in you, he who raised Christ from the dead will also give life to your mortal bodies through his Spirit who lives in you.*

This wonderful verse teaches us three things about the work of the Spirit, past, present, and future:

- It was by the Holy Spirit that Jesus was raised from the dead.
- Christians are indwelt by the Holy Spirit.
- It will be the Holy Spirit who will give life to our dead[2] bodies when we are raised from the dead.

---

[1] The Greek for 'powers' here is *dunameis*, which is used elsewhere to mean miracles (cf Acts 2:22, 1 Corinthians 12:10, Hebrews 2:4).

[2] Some have taken this to refer to divine healing on the grounds that the word used here is 'mortal', which means 'capable of death'. They argue that Paul cannot be referring to the resurrection of the body since a dead body is not mortal. It is dead! Since, therefore, a mortal body must be alive in order to be capable of death, the verse must refer to divine healing, not to resurrection. But this, in my view, does not take the context sufficiently into consideration. The parallel being drawn is with

In this way our present experience of the Holy Spirit is directly related to what the Holy Spirit will do for us in the future. Life in the Spirit now is thus both a foretaste and a guarantee of the miracle-powers of the age to come. To illustrate this, Paul uses three different metaphors, all of which say something very similar about the Spirit and the future. He sees the Spirit as a pledge, as a seal, and as firstfruits.

The Spirit as a Pledge

In 2 Corinthians 1:22, 5:5, and Ephesians 1:14 Paul refers to the Holy Spirit as a pledge. The Greek word he uses (which was originally a Hebrew word) is *arrabon.* This has a variety of meanings and no one English word is really adequate as a translation, and so it will be helpful to explore its range of meaning a little before applying it to these verses.

One interesting use of this word is to be found in the Septuagint (the Greek version of the Old Testament used at the time of Jesus and the Early Church) in Genesis 38:15-18. The details of what is a rather complicated story need not concern us here but Judah, we are told, sees a woman he thinks is a prostitute[1] and offers her a young goat from his flock as payment for sleeping with her. As he doesn't have the goat with him, the woman asks for a pledge *(arrabon)* as a

---

the *resurrection* of Christ (which Paul sees elsewhere as the firstfruits of our resurrection - 1 Corinthians 15:20, 23) and the verse points us forward to the future glory of which Paul speaks in verses 18ff - see especially v23. Furthermore, Paul's readers were alive at the time of his writing! Their bodies were, therefore, mortal. What he clearly means is that though their bodies are mortal and they will one day die, nevertheless they will ultimately be raised from the dead, the guarantee of which is their present experience of the Holy Spirit.

[1] It is noteworthy that the Bible does not, of course, commend prostitution, but it does recognise its existence. The Old Testament is, in fact, very frank about the sins of God's people.

guarantee that he will send the goat and Judah gives her his seal and its cord.

This illustration helps us to understand the general meaning of the word *arrabon*. It may be defined as *the deposit that pays part of a debt and gives a legal claim*. The seal which Judah gave Tamar as a pledge *(arrabon)* was only a small part of what he gave her but it did guarantee that she would eventually get the greater gift, the goat she had been promised. The pledge was, therefore, also *a token of a greater gift to come* and *the evidence that a promise had been made.*

Bearing this in mind it's not surprising that *arrabon* can also mean *an engagement ring.* An engagement ring is visible evidence that a promise has been made, but it also indicates that something far better is to be expected in the future. And this is very much how Paul uses *arrabon* with regard to God's gift of the Holy Spirit to the Christian. If we understand the church to be the bride of Christ (Ephesians 5:22-33), we could think of the Holy Spirit as the church's engagement ring, Christ's gift to his bride pointing forward to the day when she will be united with him at 'the wedding supper of the Lamb' (Revelation 19:7-9).

So how does all this affect our understanding of the three verses where *arrabon* is used in the New Testament? It surely backs up the idea that our present experience of the Holy Spirit is God's way of guaranteeing our future inheritance. This is clearly indicated in 2 Corinthians 1:22 where the Holy Spirit is described as *a deposit guaranteeing what is to come.* This includes the ultimate fulfillment of all God's promises (v 20) and the assurance that we will one day be given a resurrection body (2 Corinthians 5:1-5, cf Romans 8:11) and enter into our full inheritance as Christians:

Having believed, you were marked in him with a seal, the promised Holy Spirit, who is a deposit guaranteeing our inheritance until the redemption of those who are God's possession...(Ephesians 1:13-14).

But that leads us to the next closely-related theme, the Holy Spirit as a seal.

The Spirit as a Seal

The idea of the Holy Spirit as a seal *(sphragis)* is closely related to that of the Spirit as a pledge *(arrabon)*. In all three passages where *arrabon* is used (2 Corinthians 1:22, 5:5, Ephesians 1:13-14), *sphragis*[1] is used too, and even where it is used without *arrabon* it appears to have a similar meaning when it is used to refer to the Spirit (Ephesians 4:30).

Mankind has been using seals for thousands of years now and, although their use has changed relatively little, it will be helpful to mention some of the ways in which *sphragis* is used in the biblical literature. Although I am not suggesting that we are intended to understand all of these uses to apply to the work of the Spirit, any or all of them might have a bearing on our understanding of the significance of the word 'seal' in the verses referred to above.

First, it is noteworthy that a seal was used to mark an object as the property of its owner. Just as I might write my name in a book as evidence that it belongs to me, so a seal would provide evidence of ownership. It may be this that Paul has in

[1] *Sphragis* is, in fact, the noun meaning 'seal'. The verb is *sphragizo*. Although it is the verb which is used in the verses in question, I shall use the noun in order to be consistent with 'pledge' and 'firstfruits' which are also nouns. The word carries two basic meanings. It refers (1) to the instrument that makes a mark and (2) to the mark that is made by that instrument. For a detailed discussion of the use and significance of seals in ancient times, see the *sphragis* article in TDNT, Volume 7, pp939ff.

mind when he refers to Abraham's circumcision as a seal in Romans 4:11. Abraham had been given the sign of circumcision as a seal of the righteousness that he had by faith before he was circumcised. It was his faith, of course, not circumcision that made him right with God, but circumcision was the outward sign or seal that, because of his faith, he belonged to God. Similarly, when we receive the gift of the Holy Spirit that is a sure sign that we belong to God. Like Abraham we belong to God because we have believed, and *having* believed (Ephesians 1:14) we are sealed with the promised Holy Spirit[1].

Closely connected with this is the well-known use of a seal to give validity to a document. Degrees, diplomas and certificates usually carry the seal of the university or college awarding them as evidence that they are genuine, and seals are frequently used in legal documents for a similar purpose. A biblical example of this is to be found in Jeremiah 32:10ff where the prophet, having bought a field for seventeen shekels of silver, signs and seals the deed of purchase and has it witnessed. Perhaps we can learn from this that being 'sealed with the Holy Spirit' we are not only marked out as belonging

---

[1] This raises the interesting question as to whether it is the work of the Spirit at conversion (cf Chapter 5) or the baptism in the Spirit (cf Chapter 6) that seals the Christian and gives him the deposit which guarantees the things to come. In my view the natural way to read Ephesians 1:14 is to understand the sealing to *follow* the believing. Furthermore, as Stanley Horton has pointed out (op. cit. p. 239), the seal did not *cause* ownership. It only *recognised* it. It's possible to belong without being sealed, just as it's possible to be engaged without having an engagement ring! Of course born-again believers who have not been baptised in the Spirit will make it to heaven! But in my view they're certainly missing a lovely foretaste of the miracle-powers of the age to come. And if Paul appears at times to suggest that all Christians enjoy these blessings, we need to remember that in New Testament times the baptism in the Spirit was an *at/after* conversion experience (cf p. 31ff). All Christians did enjoy them then!

to God, but as, in some sense, having validity. We are the genuine article, we really do belong to him.

This leads us to another important aspect of the use of seals. If, as the principal of a college, I use the college seal to give validity to a diploma we are awarding, then I must be careful that I do not let the seal fall into the wrong hands, for whoever has that seal effectively has my authority. On the other hand, if I entrust the seal to a loyal staff-member, by giving them the seal I delegate my authority to them. This has, in fact, been a recognised use of seals for thousands of years. To hold the king's seal was to possess his authority. When Pharaoh put Joseph in charge of the whole land of Egypt he gave him a seal in the form of a signet ring (Genesis 41:41-42). The seal meant that he had Pharaoh's authority. When Jesus gave the disciples the great commission he sent them out with his authority, but he told them not to go until they had first received the Holy Spirit. There is thus a sense in which the Spirit is the source not only of our power, but of our authority as we go out into the world to preach the gospel.

Finally, a seal can be used to keep the contents of a letter secret. Sometimes envelopes are sealed with wax so that the person who receives the letter knows that no-one else has read it since it left the sender. We know from Isaiah 29:11 that even in Bible times seals were used in a similar way:

> *If you give the scroll to someone who can read, and say to him, 'Read this please', he will answer, 'I can't; it is sealed.'*

So one purpose of a seal is to keep something secret - but not for ever! When someone seals a letter it is not their intention that the letter should *never* be opened. There is always a right time for the seal to be broken. It is then that the secret is revealed.

Now Romans 8:19 tells us that the whole of creation is waiting for the sons of God to be revealed while we ourselves are waiting eagerly for our adoption as sons, *the redemption of our bodies* (v 23) and Ephesians 4:30 says that we are sealed with the Holy Spirit *for the day of redemption*.

This, together with Ephesians 1:13-14, which also speaks of our being sealed *until our redemption*, links our present experience of the Holy Spirit with that future day when the Lord himself shall descend from heaven and the dead in Christ shall rise, and when we who are alive and remain until the coming of the Lord are caught up with them to meet the Lord in the air (1 Thessalonians 4:16-17).

The *day of redemption* is the day when Jesus comes again. Paul calls it *the redemption of our bodies* (Romans 8:23) because it is on that day that our mortal bodies shall become immortal (1 Corinthians 15:50ff). Up to now the world hasn't really understood who we Christians are! It's been something of a secret. But on that day, when the entire universe shall be liberated from its bondage to decay and brought into the glorious freedom of the children of God (Romans 8:21), then the sons of God will be revealed to the whole creation. But until that day and for that day we have been sealed with the Holy Spirit.

But already we are anticipating Paul's other metaphor for the Spirit which links his present activity with that future day of redemption, the Spirit as firstfruits.

The Spirit as Firstfruits

We have already considered part of Romans 8:23 in the previous section. We must now turn our attention to a specific phrase which Paul uses here to mean something very similar to the word *arrabon* which we were considering earlier. Paul tells us that while we Christians are eagerly waiting for the redemption of our bodies we do have *the firstfruits of the Spirit.*

The Greek word for 'firstfruits' is *aparche*, and this, like *arrabon* and *sphragis,* is closely associated with the connection between our present experience of the Spirit and our future life in the kingdom of God. The concept comes from the Old Testament where we read that the *first fruits* of the harvest were to be offered to God (Exodus 23:16, 19; 34:22, 26, Leviticus 23:9ff).

It is interesting to note that Paul uses the term *firstfruits* to refer not only to the Spirit but also to Christ (1 Corinthians 15:20-23). Paul teaches us that because Christ rose from the dead we too will one day be raised. Just as the first sheaf of the harvest was offered to God in thanks for the full harvest which was to follow, so Christ was raised from the dead as a *firstfruits* of the greater resurrection when the dead in Christ shall rise. The imagery is particularly appropriate here because the day on which the sheaf of firstfruits was waved before the Lord was the day after the Sabbath following the Passover - the very day on which Jesus rose from the dead!

But how does this relate to the idea of the Spirit as *firstfruits?* Leviticus 23 is very helpful here, for a careful reading of the chapter suggests that there were in fact two occasions when *firstfruits* were offered to the Lord. The first, as we have seen, was the sheaf which was waved before the Lord on the day after the Sabbath following the Passover (Leviticus 23:11). The second was offered seven weeks later when two loaves were waved before the Lord (Leviticus 23:15-17). This took place at what was known as the Feast of Weeks and later as the Day of Pentecost[1] . It is clear that Paul is referring to this

---

[1] The word *Pentecost* comes from the Greek word for 50, representing the 50 days of the seven weeks referred to in Leviticus 23:15-16. Since

second offering of *firstfruits* when he refers in Romans 8:23 to the Spirit as *firstfruits.*

In both cases, therefore, the basic idea behind *firstfruits* is the same. The *firstfruits* were *part of* the harvest, but they were also an assurance and pledge of more to follow! So Jesus' resurrection was *part of* our resurrection and at the same time guarantees it! And the gift of the Spirit is both *part of* our inheritance in Christ (cf Ephesians 1:13-14) and at the same time points us forward to the day when that inheritance shall be ours in all its fulness.

So what can we learn from all this? We have seen that, like the symbolism of the pledge and the seal, firstfruits implies something much greater to come in the future. We have access *now* by the Spirit to the powers of the age to come (Hebrews 6:4-5), but we must recognise that we are not in that age yet! The Spirit points us future. The possession of the Spirit now is the guarantee that all God's promises will be fulfilled in the future.

This is perhaps the most appropriate way to bring this book on the Holy Spirit to a conclusion. A right understanding of the present role of the Spirit in relation to the age to come will keep us from unwise extremes. One extreme is to imagine that if we have enough faith all our problems will be solved and we can live in health, wealth and prosperity for the rest of our lives. Those who teach such things would do well to remember that we are not yet living in the age to come! Paul

---

the second *firstfruits* offering referred to in Leviticus 23 is, therefore, symbolic of the coming of the Spirit at Pentecost (as described in Acts 2), it has been suggested that the two loaves may denote the Christian church which was born at Pentecost and comprised both Jewish and Gentile believers. Such an understanding might be partly supported by James 1:18 which sees Christians as a kind of *firstfruits* of all God has created.

contrasted what he called *our present sufferings* with *the glory that shall be revealed in us* (Romans 8:18).

The other extreme is to postpone all expectation of miraculous intervention until the age to come. Such a view is equally unbalanced! It's true that we are still *groaning inwardly as we wait eagerly for our adoption as sons, the redemption of our bodies* (Romans 8:23), but the same verse makes it clear that we do have the Spirit as a *firstfruits*, as a first instalment and guarantee of our future inheritance. In receiving the Spirit we have already tasted of the miracle-powers of the coming age, and God intends us to enter in and enjoy the blessings of the Spirit now!

APPENDIX

Table illustrating different expressions used in Acts to refer to the Baptism in the Holy Spirit

See pages 124-125

The Baptism in the Holy Spirit

The table opposite shows:

1. that such expressions as *the Spirit coming upon, receiving the gift of the Holy Spirit,* and *being baptized in the Spirit* are used interchangeably in Acts as all these expressions refer to what the disciples experienced at Pentecost.

2. that the same spiritual experience is being referred to in the four passages in question as they are all examples of the Spirit *coming on* people, or, to say the same thing a different way, of people *receiving (the gift of) the Holy Spirit.*

3. that, since this experience is introduced in Acts as enduement with power for service (Acts 1:8), what the Samaritans, Cornelius, and the Ephesians received (as well as the disciples on the day of Pentecost) was their personal enduement with power.

4. that wherever Luke provides a fuller description of the Baptism in the Spirit, speaking in tongues is the first subsequent manifestation recorded. Acts thus records some 150 baptisms in the Spirit (120 + a household +12) and mentions tongues as the first result.

Please note that all references in the table are from the book of Acts. The quotations have been greatly abbreviated because of inadequate space. The best way to use the table is to consult Acts as you do so. You may also wish to compare it with what I have said in Chapter Six.

Terminology	**Pentecost**	**Samaria**	**Cornelius**	**Ephesus**
The Spirit coming on ***(epi)*** **Cf Acts 1:8** *receive power when the Holy Spirit comes on you*	**2:16-17** *This is what was spoken by the prophet.... I will pour out my Spirit on all people*	**8:16** *The Holy Spirit had not yet come on any of them*	**10:44-45** *The ...Spirit came on ......* cf **11:15** *The ....Spirit came on them*	**19:6** *The Holy Spirit came on them*
Receiving (the gift of) the Holy Spirit	**1:4** *Wait for the gift my Father promised* **2:38** *You will receive the gift of the Holy Spirit* **11:17** *God gave them the same gift as he gave us*	**8:15** *They prayed for them that they might receive the gift of the Holy Spirit* **8:17** *They received the Holy Spirit*	**10:45** *The gift of the Holy Spirit had been poured out on .....* **11:17***God gave them the same gift as he gave us*	**19:2** *Did you receive the Holy Spirit when you ...?*
Being baptized in (or with) the Holy Spirit	**1:5** *You will be baptized with the Holy Spirit*		**11:15-16** *...the Lord had said, "....you will be baptized with the Holy Spirit"*	
First manifestation recorded after Baptism in the Spirit:	**Tongues** -120 (?) people involved **2:1-4**	Incomplete description cf pp72-73	**Tongues** a household involved **10:44-46**	**Tongues** about 12 people involved **19:1-7**

Index to Scripture References

Subject Index